Life and love are two of the most discussed subjects of all time. It is no wonder that they are so prominent in the Bible. Ecclesiastes evaluates life and tells what kind of living is worthwhile; the Song of Solomon is the classic book on love. These are the two books studied in this manual. They are very different in subject, style, and purpose, as will be pointed out in the opening lesson. Your

Introduction

study of these books may bring some very refreshing surprises to you as you relate what was written almost three millenniums ago to life in the twentieth century. Remember, these two inspired books were written for *you* (2 Ti 3:16-17).

Suggestions for Study

This study manual is written to encourage independent study by the reader. The Bible is everyman's book, composed in such a manner that the average reader can comprehend its important truths for his personal light and inspiration. No greater thrill and satisfaction can come to the Bible student than to discover Bible truths himself.

Outside study aids should supplement, not supplant, independent Bible study. In addition to encouraging independent study, this manual serves as a supplementary aid to that study. There is little of commentary in the manual.[1] Rather, questions and suggestions abound. Also, the author has included a number of charts and outlines to help the reader maintain his bearing on the ocean of verses and chapters. Visual charts are valuable eye gates to new horizons.

Two of the most valuable clues to the meaning of a Bible passage which one is studying are: (*a*) seeing the relations of things: How is one word or phrase related to another word or phrase, and to the whole passage? and (*b*) recog-

---

1. Recommended commentaries are listed at the end of the book.

1

nizing emphasized truths: What is primary, and what is subordinate, in the biblical account? The emphasized truths are good clues to the main themes. The lessons of this manual keep reminding you to be looking for these clues in your study. For example, when you are directed to look for key words and phrases in the Bible text and to record them on a chart, consider this to be one of your most important activities in analysis. The basic materials of which the Bible is composed are *words*. To recognize strong words and to ponder their meaning and purpose in the midst of other words is the core of Bible study.

In determining the length of your study time, recognize your own individual situation. Sometimes one entire lesson of this manual may be one study unit. Some lessons, because of the large amount of biblical text involved, should be divided into various study units.

Further Study Reminders Applicable to all Bible Study

1. Seek *first* to learn what the Bible says. This is the step of observation. Never tire of carefully examining the Bible text. Look, look, look! ("The hearing ear, and *the seeing eye*, the LORD hath made even both of them"—Pr 20:12.) Then try to determine what the passage means—interpretation. Finally make the intended application.

2. In using this manual, observe the directions to read all Bible passages cited. Remember that your basic study is of the Bible text, not of any commentary or study guide. The Bible version referred to in this manual is the King James Version except when otherwise designated.

3. Always have pencil and paper next to your Bible as you study. The pencil is one of the best eyes. It will surprise you how many new vistas appear once you begin to record your observations on paper.

4. If you are a Christian, the Holy Spirit, who inspired the Scriptures, indwells you and offers illumination to discern the intent of the spiritual truths of the Bible. There is no better teacher of spiritual truths than the Holy Spirit. Let Him magnify Christ in the Scriptures you are studying.

5. Never fail to apply the Bible to your own life. The natural tendency is to apply it to others. Others are involved, but seek to find a personal application in the passage you are studying.

Suggestions to Leaders in Group Study

1. Tell the members of the group what they should study before coming together to discuss the lesson. Encourage faithful completion of homework, including answering of questions in the manual.

2. Do not lecture to the group. As you teach, encourage the group to ask questions and to offer comments. Plan definitely to use the latter part of your time together in discussion. Encourage everyone to participate. Honor all questions, simple or difficult, whether you are able to give a satisfactory answer or not. Let others of the group offer answers as well.

3. If possible, construct large copies of key charts of this manual, especially the survey charts, D and K. (A chalkboard or overhead projector is an excellent aid.) Keep the charts in full view before the group, using them from time to time for context reference.

4. The first part of each meeting should be devoted to a review of the previous lesson. In the last part of the meeting, summarize the lesson and encourage ways to apply the truths learned.

5. Be a good leader in setting a tone or atmosphere conducive to learning more about Christ as He is revealed by these Old Testament books. Let there be a deep conviction of the truth and authority of God's Word, and a dependency on Him for help in understanding it.

6. Let the closing prayer reflect the things you have studied in the lesson. Prayer and Bible study go hand in hand.

Publisher's Note

Enlarged charts related to the lessons of this study guide are available in *Jensen Bible Study Charts* (Vol. I, General Survey; Vol. II, Old Testament; Vol. III, New Testament). The charts are especially valuable for Bible study groups.

The $8\frac{1}{2} \times 11''$ charts can be reproduced as Xerox copies or as transparencies for overhead projectors. Selected transparencies are included in each volume.

Ecclesiastes:
Background and Survey

ECCLESIASTES IS PERPLEXING TO MANY,

PARTLY BECAUSE ITS PERSPECTIVES

AND PURPOSES ARE NOT UNDERSTOOD.

The object of this lesson is to learn what these are, by studying the book's background and making a general survey of its contents. The time you spend in this lesson will greatly help in the analytical studies that follow.

I. BACKGROUND

Not many details are known about the immediate setting of Ecclesiastes. This lack only serves to let the book shine forth in its essential quality, as a timeless and contemporary message to all generations since its writing. The things which *are* known about the book's setting are both interesting and important. Let us now look at these.

A. Title
The title for this book comes from the opening phrase, "The words of the preacher" (1:1). The word *preacher* comes from the Hebrew text thus:

Hebrew: *qoheleth*—from the root *qahal*, to assemble

Greek version: *ecclesiastes*—from *ek*, out of; and *klesis*, a calling

English: *preacher* (1:1)—one who speaks to an assembly of people

Ecclesiastes (title)—one who speaks to an assembly of people

In Old Testament days, a qoheleth was an official speaker to an assembly of people. Other appearances of the word "preacher" in Ecclesiastes are at 1:1, 2, 12; 7:17; 12:8, 9, 10. The word is not found in any other Old Testament book.

DATES OF THE WRITING OF ECCLESIASTES AND SONG OF SOLOMON

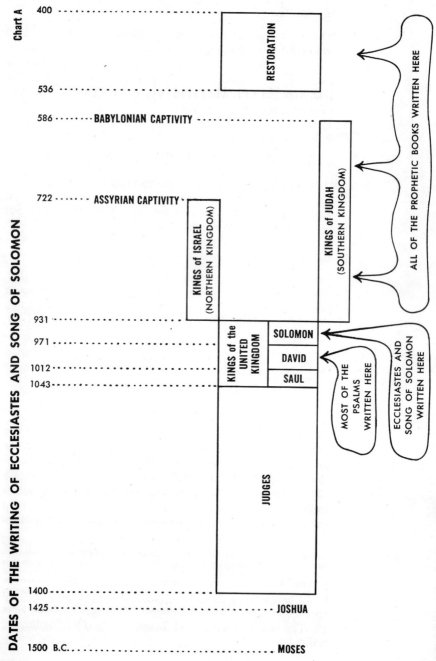

Chart A

400 ....

RESTORATION

536 ....

586 .... **BABYLONIAN CAPTIVITY** ....

722 .... **ASSYRIAN CAPTIVITY**

KINGS of ISRAEL (NORTHERN KINGDOM)

KINGS of JUDAH (SOUTHERN KINGDOM)

ALL OF THE PROPHETIC BOOKS WRITTEN HERE

931 ....

971 ....

1012 ....

1043 ....

KINGS of the UNITED KINGDOM

SOLOMON

DAVID

SAUL

MOST OF THE PSALMS WRITTEN HERE

ECCLESIASTES AND SONG OF SOLOMON WRITTEN HERE

JUDGES

1400 ....

1425 .... **JOSHUA**

1500 B.C. .... **MOSES**

6

B. Author

The author is not named in the Bible text. In 1:1 he is identified as "the son of David, king of Jerusalem." Internal evidences favor the traditional view that Solomon is meant by this phrase.[1] The following descriptions in the text coincide with what is known about Solomon from the historical record in 1 Kings.

1. the author's unrivaled wisdom (1:16)
2. his wealth (2:8)
3. his extensive building projects (2:4-6)
4. his collection of proverbs (12:9)

Chart A shows when Ecclesiastes was written, if Solomon was the author. Observe, among other things, that the preaching ministries of the Bible prophets did not begin until after Solomon's time.

C. Place in the Bible

Ecclesiastes is the fourth of five poetical books in our English Bible: Job, Psalms, Proverbs, Ecclesiastes, Song of Solomon.[2] In the Hebrew Bible it is the fourth of five megilloth writings ("five rolls"): Song of Solomon, Ruth, Lamentations, Ecclesiastes, Esther.[3] Chart B shows comparisons of some of the major subjects of the poetical books. (Lamentations is included because it is written in poetical style also.)

D. Author's Perspectives and Purposes

Throughout the book of Ecclesiastes, the author shows two opposite life views. First he views things around him as the natural man would do without the light of divine revelation. His conclusion is, "All is vanity." (Read 1 Co 2:14.) (He went through this searching experience himself sometime earlier in his career: read Ec 1:13-14.) But then the author writes as one to whom God has revealed Him-

---

1. Many commentators feel that the author lived a few hundred years after Solomon's time. See Gleason L. Archer, *A Survey of Old Testament Introduction* (Chicago: Moody, 1964), pages 462-72, for a defense of Solomonic authorship. Some hold the view that the author was an impersonator of Solomon in the book, and that he lived a few hundred years after Solomon.
2. It is interesting to observe that the historical, poetical, and prophetical sections of the Old Testament are of approximately equal length, chapter-wise: historical books, 249 chapters; poetical books: 243 chapters; prophetical books, 250 chapters.
3. Each of the five rolls was read at an annual Jewish feast. Ecclesiastes was read at the Feast of Tabernacles, which was the most joyous of the festivals.

		KEY THOUGHTS	KEY SUBJECTS
3 DIDACTIC BOOKS	PROVERBS	WISDOM	Description and fruits of the righteous man
	ECCLESIASTES	FUTILITY	The way to God
	JOB	TRIAL	Crucible of testing
3 DEVOTIONAL BOOKS	PSALMS	WORSHIP	Meditations and worship of the righteous man
	SONG OF SOLOMON	LOVE	The way of God
	LAMENTATIONS	DESTRUCTION	Crucible of judgment

self, and now his observations and conclusions have the ring of surety and hope. For example: "whatsoever God doeth, it shall be for ever" (3:14). This pattern of alternating perspectives continues throughout the book, as we shall see in the survey study of this lesson.

It should be observed that when the author of Ecclesiastes writes from the second perspective noted above, it is not as one who knows God from full revelation. He views life as a man does who knows and worships God primarily as Creator. This is confirmed by the fact that every time he names Him, he uses the word *Elohim*, which is the name especially associated with the work of creation (cf. Gen 1:1). The name *Lord* (Jehovah), which is the Old Testament equivalent of Redeemer-Saviour, does not appear once in the book.[4] Today when the reader of Ecclesiastes

4. Read Exodus 5:22—6:9 for the significance of this covenant-name, *Jehovah* (KJV, Lord). Solomon refers to Jehovah often in the book of Proverbs, so it is not that he himself did not know God as Lord. If Ecclesiastes was composed after Proverbs, Solomon is recalling his search for meaning-in-life before he came to know God as His Redeemer (cf. 1:13). Some maintain that he wrote from a backslidden spiritual condition.

reaches the last command of the book, "Fear God, and keep his commandments" (12:13), he is ready to be introduced to Christ the Redeemer. "As the law was designed to lead men to Christ, so this book was written to lead those 'under the sun' to the Son (cf. Heb. 1:1)."[5]

The purposes of Ecclesiastes, then, are to show the futility of pursuing materialistic, earthly goals as an end in themselves, and to point to God as the source of all that is truly good.[6] The theme of the book is determined by those purposes, and may be stated in this twofold way:

(1.) Every pursuit of man is futile if God is excluded.
(2.) Only God's work endures, so that only He can impart true value to man's life and service.

E. Style

Job, Proverbs, Ecclesiastes, and parts of other Old Testament books are classified as wisdom literature. The style of these books is that of the philosopher, who shares his observations, reflections, reasonings, and conclusions in terse and brief lines, often in poetical form. Here is one writer's evaluation of Ecclesiastes' composition:

> Whether prose or verse, I know nothing grander in its impassioned survey of mortal pain and pleasure, its estimate of failure and success.[7]

F. Ecclesiastes and Philosophy

The dictionary defines philosophy as the investigation of causes and laws underlying reality. Stated simply, philosophy is man's search for truth. Throughout the book of Ecclesiastes, Solomon presents the position of one who is searching for truth and reality and meaning. From this standpoint, then, it would be correct to say that Ecclesiastes is a book of philosophy.

Generally speaking, there are two main schools of thought in philosophy: empiricism and rationalism. Empiricism says that human experience, especially of the senses, is the only source of knowledge. That is, man can

---

5. Wick Broomall, "Ecclesiastes," in *The Zondervan Pictorial Bible Dictionary*, p. 232.
6. A marginal note of NASB suggests the word *futility* as a translation of "vanity" (1:2). This is the word which will be used most of the time by this manual.
7. E. C. Stedman, quoted by W. Graham Scroggie, *Know Your Bible* (London: Pickering & Inglish, 1940), 1:144.

know only what he experiences. Rationalism says that human reason is the prime source of knowledge and of spiritual truth. That is, man can know only what he can mentally grasp. It is interesting to observe in Ecclesiastes that truth is sought for in both ways:

"I made," "I got," etc. (2:4, 7)—*empiricism*

"I gave my heart to know" (1:17)—*rationalism*

The conclusion in both quests is stated over and over again: "all is vanity." That frustration serves to show that if truth is to be known, it must come by revelation from God. (See diagram.) The God-centered life view which Solomon teaches in the book came from divine revelation.

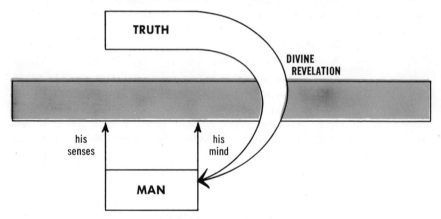

It must have been an interesting experience to be personally acquainted with the man Solomon in the early days of Israel. Here was a man upon whom God lavished so many gifts and talents. He was a musician, poet, botanist, zoologist, businessman, administrator, and king. His "wisdom excelled the wisdom of all the children of the east country, and all the wisdom of Egypt" (1 Ki 4:30). No wonder people traveled from all parts of the world to his palace to see and hear him. This was the man whom God chose to write a large portion of His inspired Scripture: Ecclesiastes, Song of Solomon, Proverbs, and two psalms (72, 127). So although we did not live in the days of famous Solomon, we have the privilege today to read and study his choicest writings, which excel all others penned by him, because they are uniquely and infallibly inspired, wholly trustworthy.

II. SURVEY

Now you are ready to study the actual text of Ecclesiastes. Before you begin to analyze each chapter in detail, however, it is very important that you first view the book as a whole—in a panoramic survey or overview. This will show you such things as general theme, perspectives, and highlights of the book. Survey of this kind will help you later to analyze accurately with broad context in mind.

A. First Readings

Scan Ecclesiastes once or twice, catching its tone and large emphases. What are your impressions after this first reading? (Note: Do not tarry over details in this scanning stage, or you might lose sight of the broad panorama.)

B. Further Readings

Your next readings should be in shorter portions, at a slower pace. But keep in mind that you are still in the survey stage of study. Here are some suggestions for study. 1. Chart C divides the book of Ecclesiastes into eleven sections of varying lengths. The reasons for divisions at the verses indicated will be evident as you proceed with your survey study. For now, mark these divisions in your Bible. It is recommended that you draw a line across the page of your Bible at the beginning of each divisional point. This is a big aid in study.
2. What repeated words and phrases have you already observed in the text of Ecclesiastes? Keep looking for

DIVISIONAL POINTS OF THE BOOK OF ECCLESIASTES   Chart C

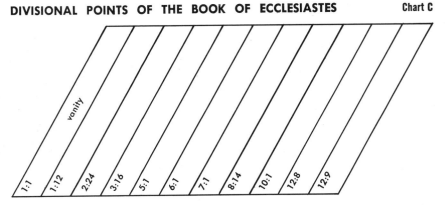

11

others during the remainder of the lesson. Three key examples are "vanity," "under the sun," and "God." Read through the book and underline or circle these words every time they appear. Use a different colored pencil for each, for this will help you see groupings of the phrases. Such groupings or concentrations are clues to emphasis. The importance of these phrases are indicated by their many appearances in the book:

vanity—39 times
under the sun—29 times
God—40 times

3. Read 1:14 and note the close relation between "under the sun" and "vanity." The phrase *under the sun* refers to the earthbound, temporal outlook and experience of the natural man, and this is vanity, or futility. So in Ecclesiastes the phrases *under the sun* and *vanity* refer to the same thought. The opposite outlook, the hopeful one, is that which looks toward God, who is above the sun. With this in mind, scan your marked Bible, with its markings of the key phrases noted above. Observe which sections are about God more than they are about vanity, and which are about vanity more than about God. Record your findings below. (An example is given.)

SECTION	EMPHASIS
1:1-11	vanity
1:12—2:23	
2:24—3:15	God
3:16—4:16	
5:1-20	
6:1-12	
7:1—8:13	
8:14—9:18	
10:1—12:7	
12:8	
12:9-14	

What pattern or order do you observe here? Record the words *vanity* and *God* in the appropriate spaces on Chart C (example shown). •

4. Compare 1:2 and 12:8. Since these similar verses appear at the beginning and end of the book, what do they suggest is a prominent theme of the chapters in between?

5. Read 1:1-11. How does the section serve as an introduction to the book?

6. Read 12:9-14. How do these verses conclude the book?

C. Survey Chart

Chart D is a survey chart of Ecclesiastes, showing how the book is organized, thought-wise.[8] Refer to it as you follow each of the suggestions given below.

1. Note how the introduction (1:1-11) is identified. The premise, or proposition, that "all is futility" is restated in the conclusion, at 12:8.

2. The main body of the book is 1:12—12:7. Observe on the chart that this is divided into four sermons. These sermons of the preacher could also be called discourses of the teacher. Each sermon expounds on two subjects: futility (vanity), and hope. In other words, in each sermon Solomon first shows the hopelessness of life where the outlook is earthbound ("under the sun"); and then he shows that real hope is founded only on God, whose dwelling place is beyond the heavens. Compare this repeated alternation (vanity; God) in the four sermons with the observations you recorded on Chart C.

3. Observe what is recorded in the oblique spaces on Chart D. The first part of each sermon is mainly observation, where the preacher tells what he, as a natural man, saw. Hence the repeated phrase in these sections, *I saw* (e.g. 4:7). The second part of each sermon also includes observation, but it is mainly instruction and counsel about things of God.

4. Note how the conclusion (12:8-14) is a condensed summary of the four sermons:

8. Various outlines have been made of Ecclesiastes. Some expositors feel there is no organization of thought, that the book is "disjointed in construction" (G. S. Hendry, "Ecclesiastes," in *The New Bible Commentary,* p. 538). The position of this manual is that there is a discernible pattern of thought, developed in four sermons, shown on Chart D.

ECCLESIASTES   VANITY UNDER THE SUN; HOPE IN GOD

KEY VERSES
1:14; 3:14

KEY WORDS
vanity
under the sun
wisdom
God
vexation of spirit
labor
evil
know

introduction	OBSERVATIONS, CONCLUSIONS, AND COUNSEL	conclusion

conclusion
INSTRUCTION AND COUNSEL
OBSERVATION
12:14

SUMMARY OF THE SOLUTION

FEAR GOD

all is vanity
12:8

PREMISE RESTATED

12:9

FOURTH SERMON   PROVERBS
Remember   10:1
under the sun   8:14

11:1   REMEMBRANCE OF GOD

FUTILITY

THIRD SERMON
fear God   7:1
I saw vanity   6:1

KNOWLEDGE OF GOD

FUTILITY

SECOND SERMON
God is in heaven   5:1
I saw vanity   3:16

5:18   GIFT FROM GOD
5:8   FUTILITY

WORSHIP OF GOD

FUTILITY

FIRST SERMON
fear before him   2:24
seek and search out   1:12

PURPOSE WITH GOD

FUTILITY

all is vanity   1:1

PREMISE (1:14) ALL IS FUTILITY

"WHATSOEVER GOD DOETH, IT SHALL BE FOREVER" (3:14)

14

Part One: observation—All is vanity. (12:8)
Part Two: instruction and counsel—Fear God. (12:9-14)

5. Lists of proverbs appear at a couple of places in the book. Chapter 10 is an example. Note how this is identified on Chart D.

6. Observe the key words listed on the chart. Read the two key verses which are also cited. How are these reflected in the title assigned to the book?

D.   A Study of the Topic of Vanity

Read the following selected verses as an introduction to the subject of vanity in this book.[9]

THE TEN VANITIES			
Human wisdom	2:15-16	Human fame	4:16
Human labor	2:19-21	Human insatiety	5:10
Human purpose	2:26	Human coveting	6:9
Human rivalry	4:4	Human frivolity	7:6
Human avarice	4:7	Human awards	8:10, 14

Some Review Questions

1. What Hebrew word does the title *Ecclesiastes* translate? What is the literal meaning of that Hebrew word?

2. What are some evidences that Solomon was the writer of Ecclesiastes?

3. If Solomon wrote this book, was it before or after the Old Testament prophets?

4. If Ecclesiastes were written after the time of most of the Old Testament prophets, would you expect the book to reflect something of the prophets' Messianic message? Does Ecclesiastes present such a message?

5. What is the twofold theme of Ecclesiastes? How is this twofold message developed in the pattern of the whole book?

6. How many "sermons" appear in Ecclesiastes? What are the two main subjects of those sermons?

7. Compare the introduction and conclusion of the book.

9.   The list is from J. Sidlow Baxter, *Explore The Book* (Grand Rapids: Zondervan, 1960), 3:163. Used by permission.

8. Define philosophy, empiricism, and rationalism. What do these terms have to do with the message of Ecclesiastes?

9. Name some key words of Ecclesiastes. Can you recall the main point of each of the two key verses chosen for the book?

10. What title would you give to the book of Ecclesiastes?

All Is Vanity

KING DAVID'S SON WAS A PREACHER;

HIS MESSAGE WAS DARK AND BLEAK:

"ALL IS VANITY UNDER THE SUN!"

One would expect to hear such a cry from a disillusioned soul who knows not God. But would a preacher sent from God address a congregation that way? If so, why? These are some of the questions which we will want answered from the text of the Bible itself. One thing is certain at this point: the author used the element of surprise in his opening wail about vanity (1:2).

I. PREPARATION FOR STUDY

The Hebrew word translated "vanity" is *hebel,* and means something transitory, passing swiftly away (cf. Ja 4:14, "vapor"). The word appears in various books of the Old Testament. Read the following selected references: 2 Kings 17:15; Job 7:16; Psalm 39:4-6; Proverbs 13:11; Isaiah 57:13; Jeremiah 51:17-18. Note especially how the Psalms and Jeremiah passages use the word. Psalm 39:5 interprets clearly Solomon's burden:[1] "Every man at his best state is altogether vanity." Whenever the word *futility* is used in this manual to represent the word *vanity,* the meaning of *transitoriness* (impermanence) is included in the interpretation. Here is an illustration: "The suggestions which we made at the peace table were futile, for we accomplished nothing."

1. Throughout this manual the name Solomon will be used as the writer of Ecclesiastes. Even if you hold that another man wrote the book, this frequent reference to Solomon should not distract you.

II. ANALYSIS

Segment to be analyzed: 1:1-11
Stanza divisions:[2] at verses 1, 4, 8. Mark these in your
   Bible.

A. General Analysis

Read the entire passage as a unit. What are your impressions? If you have access to the New American Standard Bible, note how this version prints verses 2-11 line by line, in poetry form. This is a valuable aid for analysis.

B. Stanza Analysis

PARAGRAPH 1:1-3. Introduction and Theme
1. What three words of the first verse identify the position

and ministry of the author? _____

What responsibilities rested upon him? _____

_____

2. The emphasis of verse 2 is obvious. If you were saying
something like this to a person today, how would you say
it? (Recall the meaning of the word *vanity* as discussed

earlier in the lesson.) _____

_____

_____

3. The observation and conclusion of verse 2 leads to the
question and problem of verse 3. How would you ask the

question of verse 3 in your own words? _____

_____

In what sense does the word *all* (1:3) show how intense

the problem is? _____

_____

STANZA 1:4-7. Life Is So Transitory
1. Each of the four verses is about a different subject. (See
Notes on verse 4.) Underline in your Bible the four words

2. Most of Ecclesiastes is in prose form, where the unit of thought is the
paragraph. In the poetic sections (e.g. 1:2-11), we will use the designation
stanza for such units.

18

introducing the four subjects. What common observation is made about all four? _____

_____

2. How do these verses illustrate the statement of 1:2 that "all is transitory"?[3] _____

_____

3. Is Solomon implying by these verses that something is wrong about this circular pattern of nature? If not, what is he trying to say? _____

STANZA 1:8-11. Life Is So Monotonous
1. In the preceding stanza, Solomon's illustrations were from nature, showing its circular pattern. Now he takes his illustrations from history, where man is the main participant. Read the stanza. (See *Notes* on verse 8.) What is the main point? _____
2. Is Solomon implying that it is wrong for history to repeat itself? If not, what is he implying? _____

_____

III. NOTES

1. "What profit hath a man?" (1:3). That is, "What advantage does man have in all his work which he does under the sun?" (NASB). This is the dark view of the natural man:

> The natural man is unaware that all the affirmative answers to life are to be found in Him Who is above, not "under the sun." The natural man grovels in the dust and finds only earthworms, while the spiritual man may soar up with wings as eagles, above all that is futile and disappointing, and live in the consciousness of God's companionship, favor and incomparable, everlasting rewards.[4]

3. Although the word vanity in 1:2 is a noun, it is occasionally paraphrased in this manual by an adjective (e.g. "transitory"), merely to avoid awkward expression (e.g. "all is transitoriness").
4. *The Amplified Bible*, p. 743 note.

2. "But the earth abideth for ever" (1:4). The emphasis of the verse is not on the abiding character of the earth, but on the transient character of generations, *while* the earthly setting remains.

3. "The sun . . . ariseth, and the sun goeth down" (1:5). This is not an inaccurate scientific statement, but phenomenal language, describing what *appears* to the viewer. It is the earth's motion (rotation), not the sun's, which is responsible for this sight, but from man's view it appears that the sun is the object moving, and so the description is from that perspective. If Solomon had known and described the correct astronomical movements, his readers, whose knowledge was based only on appearance, would only have been confused. Every daily newspaper perpetutates this supposed scientific blunder by reporting the times of sunrise and sunset!

4. "The wind goeth toward the south" (1:6). This verse describes very accurately the trajectory of winds in a storm system of the northern hemisphere, just as verse 7 describes the unending water cycle of cloud-rain-river-ocean-evaporation-cloud. But Solomon was not attempting to give scientific descriptions in these verses, even if he had the knowledge. Rather, he was describing *appearance* (just as verse 5). In the case of verses 6 and 7, the language is that of both appearance and scientific factuality.

5. "All things are full of labor" (1:8). Berkeley Version paraphrases the first half of verse 8 thus: "All things are unspeakably tiresome."

IV. FOR THOUGHT AND DISCUSSION

1. Reflect some more on the key phrase, "All is vanity." Recall the discussion about it in lesson 1. Are these the words of a pessimist or a realist? If neither, how would you identify the person speaking?

2. Life is very transitory, as suggested by the statement, "One generation passeth away, and another generation cometh" (1:4). What spiritual lessons can be derived from this truth?

3. Read 1 John 2:17. Does this conflict with the words, "the earth abideth for ever" (Ec 1:4)? What is meant by *world* in that context?

4. What are your thoughts about the statement, "There is no new thing under the sun" (1:9)? Read 2 Peter 3:3-7. What is the error of forcing the status quo principle upon all things in all times? Does history repeat itself always?

5. What are your reactions to the contemporary scene's new morality, new theology, new music? If you are studying with a group, you may want to discuss the doctrinal errors of neoorthodoxy (new orthodoxy).[5]

6. Can you think of references in the Bible to things new (e.g. new convenant)? Consult a concordance for references, especially in the book of Revelation.

7. What is lacking in the heart of a person who is never satisfied (1:8)? Is human *desire* normal or abnormal? What is the solution to the inner cravings of an unsatisfied soul?

8. Can your generation leave something good for the next generation? Is this contradicted by 1:11? Compare a modern paraphrase of 1:11. What works are not enduring? Compare Psalm 49:11.

9. Why do writers of Scripture often use language of appearance (phenomenal language) rather than exact scientific terminology? If you were living in New York, why would you describe a trip to Florida as "going down to Florida"? Many of the physical cataclysms of last times as described in Revelation will surely involve nuclear activity. Does it surprise you not to find phrases like *atomic fall-out* in Revelation?

V. FURTHER STUDY

Make an extended study of the subject mentioned earlier about new things in the Bible. Does the fact of newness imply change of mind? For example, did God change His mind by making a new covenant? (Jer 31:31)?

VI. WORDS TO PONDER

And I saw a new heaven and a new earth (Rev 21:1).

---

5. See Charles Ryrie, *Neo-Orthodoxy* (Chicago: Moody, 1956), for a discussion of this subtle theology.

First Sermon:
Bring God into the Picture

THE PASSAGE OF THIS LESSON IS

THE FIRST SERMON DELIVERED BY

THE PREACHER OF JERUSALEM.

It is his testimony of once having searched everywhere for enduring values in life, and eventually having found them in God. The audience of the preacher is made up of the pessimists and fatalists whose complaint has already been registered in the book: "All is vanity" (1:2). The preacher agrees that all is vanity, but that it is so only to one who has not come to see and know God, and who refuses to bring God into the picture of his life.

I. PREPARATION FOR STUDY

1. Review the survey Chart D, observing how 1:12—3:15 is represented in the structure of the book. Note that the sermon is of two parts: negative (futility) (1:12—2:23); and positive (purpose) (2:24—3:15).
2. Recall from your survey study of Lesson 1 that the name *God* appears in clusters from time to time in the book. If you have marked these occurrences in the pages of your Bible, you will note that there is a cluster in the second part of this first sermon (2:24—3:15).[1] (Mark these now, if you have not already done so.)

II. ANALYSIS

Segment to be analyzed: 1:12—3:15
Paragraph divisions: at verses 1:12; 2:1, 12, 18, 24; 3:1, 9.

Mark these in your Bible.

1. In Ecclesiastes the name *God* appears only once before this time (at 1:13).

A. General Analysis

1. Read the passage paragraph by paragraph, and record a main theme for each:

1:12-18 _____

2:1-11 _____

2:12-17 _____

2:18-23 _____

2:24-26 _____

3:1-8 _____

3:9-14 _____

2. Were you able to detect a different tone in the passage when you reached the place where Solomon begins to speak about God (2:24 ff.)? Why should a person's outlook

change when he brings God into the picture? _____

_____

The following diagram illustrates this contrasting picture which appears throughout Ecclesiastes:[2]

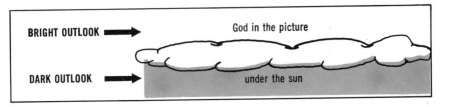

3. Chart E is a survey of this segment. Observe how the segment is divided into two main parts. Note also how each paragraph is identified by a main subject. Compare this outline with your paragraph themes which you recorded earlier in the lesson. Try to justify the choice of each word in the outline, beginning with "intellect."

4. Use the blank spaces on Chart E to record various observations which you will be making as you proceed with

2. When isolated as a symbol, the word *sun* suggests brightness. But the idiom *under the sun* is merely a symbol of location and means "earthbound."

under the sun						God in the picture	
ALL IS VANITY						EVERYTHING IS BEAUTIFUL	

1:12   2:1   2:12   2:18   2:24   3:1   3:9   3:15

INTELLECT	PLEASURE	PREEMINENCE	PRODUCTION	BASIC ENJOYMENTS	APPROPRIATE TIMES	WORKS OF GOD

your study. Keep in mind that even the recording of an isolated word can be the starter of a significant study.

B. Paragraph Analysis

UNDER THE SUN (1:12—2:23)
This is the dark side of the preacher's first sermon. It is the story of one who seeks but does not find.

PARAGRAPH 1:12-18. Intellect Is Not the Key to Life
What was it that Solomon had set out to search for (1:13)?

_____

_____

What path did he follow in this quest, according to this

paragraph? _____

_____

Observe how often the words *wisdom* and *knowledge* are repeated here. Would you say that they determine the emphasis of the paragraph?

Read 1 Kings 3:12; 4:30-31; 10:23-24 for the historical record of the unsurpassed wisdom of Solomon. Since he was the wisest of all, how significant was it that he gave such a pessimistic evaluation of the fruits of wisdom (Ec

1:18)? _____

Verse 14 is one of the key verses of the book. (See survey Chart D.) Are the works those of God or of men? Verse 15 points to the impotency of someone. Is it of God, or of man?

PARAGRAPH 2:1-11. Pleasure Is Not the Key to Life
Read the paragraph and make a list of the various possessions and experiences which Solomon claimed as his own. Did Solomon find any pleasure or enjoyment in these? (See 2:10.) If he did, then account for his dark judgment

expressed in verses 1, 2, and 11. _____

_____

Note Solomon's testimony of 2:9 that even during his pursuit of pleasure he remained a wise man. What does this

teach, in view of 1:12-18? _____

_____

PARAGRAPH 2:12-17. Preeminence Is Not the Key to Life
Solomon knew that he excelled over most men in virtually every area of life (e.g. wisdom, riches, honor). How does

he claim this distinction in verses 12-14a? _____

_____

But what did Solomon observe which disturbed him (vv.

14b-16)? _____

_____

How do the words "Therefore I hated life" strike you?

_____

_____

PARAGRAPH 2:18-23. Production Is Not the Key to Life
Solomon did not devote all his time spending and consuming things. He also kept building, investing, and producing. But therein lay a vexing problem to him. What was the problem? See verses 18 and 21. _____

_____

How often is the word *labor* repeated in this paragraph?

_____

GOD IN THE PICTURE (2:24—3:15)
At this point in the sermon, the preacher moves to the positive theme that there is purpose in life if God is in the picture. "True enjoyment is possible, but it does not lie within man's power to bestow it upon himself."[3]

PARAGRAPH 2:24-26. True Enjoyment Is from God
Use the following translation of verses 24-25:

> It is not a good thing **inherent** in man that he is able to eat and drink and get satisfaction in his toil. This, too, have I seen that such a thing is entirely from the hand of God. For who can eat, and who can have enjoyment apart from Him?[4]

Solomon recognizes that true enjoyment is possible, but he emphasizes that its source is where? _____

_____

How often does the word *give* appear in 2:26? What is the point of the verse? _____
Does the last sentence ("This also is vanity—") refer to the whole paragraph, or to the sinner's lot, "travail" (2:26)?

PARAGRAPH 3:1-8. There Is an Appointed Time for Everything
Read these verses for first impressions. How does the whole stanza strike you: as optimistic, pessimistic, fatalistic, realistic, or a combination of any of these? _____

_____

3. H. C. Leupold, *Exposition of Ecclesiastes*, p. 76.
4. Ibid., p. 74.

Are all the pairs of the list made up of contrasts? What type of contrast is common to all? _____

_____

What phrase of the verses is repeated most often? _____

_____

How does the pair of 3:2a introduce the whole list? _____

_____

How is it different from the other pairs? _____

_____

What do you think is the purpose of this stanza? _____

_____

Compare your conclusions with these two different purposes:
(a) to emphasize the sovereignty of God in all aspects of a person's life
(b) to show that life is continually made up of options, and that every hour is an hour of decision

PARAGRAPH 3:9-15. God's Works Are Beautiful
How many times does the name *God* appear here? _____
This paragraph teaches many deep and wonderful truths about God and His works. Study the verses carefully, and list these truths below.

_____

_____

_____

_____

_____

III. NOTES

1. "Vexation of spirit" (1:14). The Hebrew word translated "spirit" means literally wind, or breath. This is the reason for the Berkeley Version reading, "chasing of

wind." This figurative expression is very appropriate in Ecclesiastes, where the note of futility is underscored.

2. "The world in their heart" (3:11). Most modern versions translate *the world* as "eternity."

3. "No man can find out" (3:11). Leupold writes,

> Man has a deep-seated "sense of eternity," of purposes and destinies. Yet even then he is not able fully to master the problem, for the reach of eternity involved is too vast for him.[5]

4. "No good in them, but for a man" (3:12). These words are better translated by the New American Standard Bible: "nothing better for them than."

5. "God requireth that which is past" (3:15). Various translations or paraphrases have been made of this part of the verse. Compare these:

> "God seeks what has passed by" (NASB).
> "God seeks what has been driven away" (RSV).
> "God brings to pass again what was in the distant past and disappeared" (TLB).

IV. FOR THOUGHT AND DISCUSSION

1. "He that increaseth knowledge increaseth sorrow" (1:18). Have you ever observed this to be true? If so, account for such a consequence. Is knowledge, of itself, evil?

2. Pleasure is the god of multitudes today. Is this hedonistic outlook worldwide? Note that it was one of the five causes identified by Edward Gibbon as bringing about the fall of the Roman Empire in the early centuries:

(*a*) the rapid increase in divorce and the breakdown of the family
(*b*) soaring taxes
(*c*) the mad craze for pleasure
(*d*) gigantic armaments
(*e*) decay of religion[6]

3. One television star divorced his wife because his home obligations were competing with his career. In his own words, he was "trapped by success." What are your reactions?

4. When the final examination grades at Cambridge Uni-

---

5. Ibid., p. 91.
6. Edward Gibbon, *The Decline and Fall of the Roman Empire*, 3 vols. (New York: Modern Library, n.d.).

versity were published, Henry Martyn's highest ambition had been realized. He was the honors man of the year. Strangely, his first sensation was keen disappointment. "I obtained my highest wishes," he said, "but was surprised that I had grasped a shadow." What are your highest ambitions in life?

5. "Thou hast made me for Thyself, and my heart will not rest until it rests in Thee." Compare this statement by Augustine with Ecclesiastes 2:25b, "Who can have enjoyment without Him?" (NASB).

V. FURTHER STUDY

1. As noted in lesson 1, Ecclesiastes was the book read by Jews at their Feast of Tabernacles. This was their most joyous feast, celebrating the harvest of grapes, figs and olives. Why do you suppose a book like Ecclesiastes, with its many pessimistic portions, was chosen for that occasion? Consider 2:24 ff. in answering this.

2. The word *heart* is found forty times in Ecclesiastes. It first appears at 1:13. The heart is the seat of a person's thoughts and actions, whether good or bad. Study the following passages and record your observations of this subject. (The physical heart is not meant by these references. What is meant?)

References	The heart is the seat of:
Mt 5:28; 2 Pe 2:14	
Mt. 9:4; Heb 4:12	
Mt 13:15; Ro 1:21	
Mk 2:6; Lk 24:38	
Mk 11:23; Ro 10:10; Heb 3:12	
Lk 1:51	
Lk 24:32; Ac 21:13	
Jn 12:40; Eph 4:18	

Jn 14:1; Ro 9:2; 2 Co 2:4	
Jn 16:22; Eph 5:19	
Ac 2:37; 1 Jn 3:20	
Ac 11:23; 2 Co 9:7	
Ro 6:17; Col 3:15	
Heb 4:12; cf. 1 Pe 4:1	

3. Read Psalm 49 and observe that David was faced with the same dilemmas as Solomon. What were some of David's solutions?

VI. WORDS TO PONDER

That which is crooked cannot be made straight (Ec 1:15).

The crooked shall be made straight . . . and
all flesh shall see the salvation of God (Lk 3:5-6).

Second Sermon: God Is in Heaven

THE PREACHER HAS MORE TO SHARE

OF WHAT HE HAS OBSERVED

AND EXPERIENCED IN LIFE.

The theme of this second sermon is basically the same as that of the first, underscoring the futility of an earthbound life-view, and the vitality of a personal relation to God. But while the theme is the same, the illustrations, teachings, and exhortations are new and fresh. What reader, for example, does not.pause and reflect when he comes upon these awesome words in the text: "God is in heaven, and thou upon earth" (5:2)?

What things do you value highly in life? Are they permanent? Do you think God wants you to really enjoy life? How big is your faith in God? The passage of this lesson should stir you to consider aspects of your own personal life suggested by such questions.

I. PREPARATION FOR STUDY

1. Review the survey Chart D. Note that this second sermon treats the two-part theme twice, making a total of four parts:

3:16—4:16	Futility
5:1-7	Worship of God
5:8-17	Futility
5:18-20	Gift from God

2. Recall the title assigned to the book of Ecclesiastes: "Vanity under the sun; hope in God." If Ecclesiastes did not include the second part of the theme, do you think it would be part of the Bible?

3. Mark in your Bible the substitute readings of the text, shown in *Notes*. Use these as you proceed with your study.

II. ANALYSIS

Segment to be analyzed: 3:16—5:20
Paragraph divisions: at verses 3:16; 4:1, 4, 7, 13; 5:1, 4, 8, 10, 13, 18. Mark these in your Bible.

A. General Analysis

1. Read the segment in one sitting, for overall impressions.
2. If you have not already done so, underline or circle in your Bible the following words as they appear in the passage: vanity, under the sun, God. Do you observe any clusters of the repeated name *God*?
3. Chart F is a survey of this segment. At this time do not study the paragraph outline shown in the oblique spaces. Observe the four-part outline at the top of the chart. You may want to record this outline in your Bible.
4. Read each paragraph and determine a theme for each. Compare your conclusions with the outline of Chart F shown in the oblique spaces.

SECOND SERMON: Chart F
God Is in Heaven (3:16—5:20)

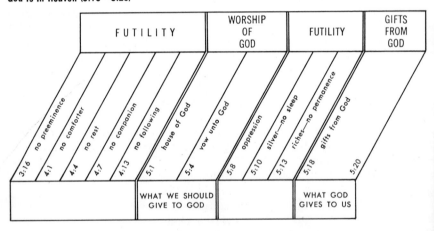

B. Paragraph Analysis

A few selected questions about each paragraph are given below. You may want to inquire more into the content of the paragraphs.

FUTILITY

PARAGRAPH 3:16-22. No Preeminence
With whom is man compared here? Is the comparison true?

_____

What is there about man that makes him appear beastly?
(3:16-18) _____

What doubt is expressed in verse 21? _____

_____

Verse 22 should be interpreted in light of that doubt. (The word *wherefore* of verse 22 means "therefore" in this context.)

PARAGRAPH 4:1-3. No Comforter

What two groups are cited as without comforters? _____

_____

What are your reactions to the pessimistic view of 4:2-3?

_____

PARAGRAPH 4:4-6. No Rest

What kind of rivalry is suggested by verse 4? _____

_____

Do you agree with the proverb of verse 6? _____

PARAGRAPH 4:7-12. No Companion
(Note: Verses 7-8 continue the theme of Ecclesiastes. Verses 9-12 are a parenthesis of proverbs about the subject introduced by verse 8.)

What situation of futility is suggested by 4:8? _____

_____

Have you ever heard of rich misers who have withdrawn from society and have lived in virtual poverty?

PARAGRAPH 4:13-16. No Following
Verse 15b refers to a young successor to the aged king of

4:13. Is the young king eventually rejected (4:16)? _____

_____

Is popularity a fickle and transient commodity? What does
it depend on? _____

Why is this also "vanity and vexation of spirit"? _____

_____

WORSHIP OF GOD

PARAGRAPH 5:1-3. House of God
What various truths about true worship do you learn from

this paragraph? _____

_____

_____

_____

What attitude or frame of mind is emphasized here? _____

_____

Why is it so important to listen to the voice of God? _____

_____

Compare these three dwelling places of God: house, heart,

heaven. _____

_____

_____

PARAGRAPH 5:4-7. Vow unto God

What do you learn here about making vows to God? _____

_____

What is a vow? _____
Should vows be voluntary? Compare Deuteronomy 23:21-
22. Do you make vows to God? If so, what are they, and

how often do you make them? _____

_____

What strong command is given at the end of this para-

graph? _____

_____

FUTILITY

The preacher now returns to the original premise about futility. The next three paragraphs are about hopeless situations involving money.

PARAGRAPH 5:8-9. Oppression of the Poor
Refer to modern versions and commentaries for help in interpreting the meaning of this paragraph. Also see *Notes*.

PARAGRAPH 5:10-12. No Sleep

Why do riches often rob a person of sleep? _____

_____

PARAGRAPH 5:13-17. No Permanence
(See *Notes* for a paraphrase of 5:13b.)
What is basically evil about hoarding one's riches (5:13-

14)? _____
Compare Jesus' parable of the hidden talent (Mt 25:14-30).

GIFTS FROM GOD
The preacher's sermon ends on a positive note, with references to good gifts from God.

PARAGRAPH 5:18-20. What God Gives to Us

Compare verse 18 with 2:22 and 3:22. _____

_____

What does verse 18 include, not found in the other verses?

_____

What gifts from God are mentioned here? _____

_____

Compare this with the subject of 5:1-7 (What We Should Give to God). See Chart F.

III. NOTES

1. "Angel" (5:6). Both the Hebrew and Greek words translated *angel* mean literally "messenger," whether heavenly or earthly. Most often the references in the Bible are to heavenly beings. In this verse the messenger is a minister

or official of the temple, possibly the priest, who collected the money which had been pledged to God (cf. Mal 2:7). 2. "He that is higher than the highest" (5:8). *The Wycliffe Bible Commentary* interprets the setting as one of graft and corruption:

> This is not a statement to the effect that God watches all earthly rulers, and will eventually punish them, but rather it refers to the system of government in those days. Each official watched the one beneath him in order to obtain part of the spoils of taxation and graft. Because of this system one should not marvel [v. 8] at the oppression and lack of justice.[1]

3. Use the following substitute readings of the Bible text to help clarify some obscure phrases of the King James Version.

King James Reading	Substitute Reading
3:16 place of judgment	place of justice
21 Who knoweth the spirit of man that	Who knoweth whether the spirit of man
4: 8 There is one alone, and there is not a second	There is a man without a dependent
5: 1 Keep thy foot	Guard your steps
6 the angel	the messenger
13 riches kept for the owners	riches hoarded by their owners
14 riches perish by evil travail	riches are lost through bad investment
20a remember the days	consider the years
20b God answereth him	God keeps him occupied

IV. FOR THOUGHT AND DISCUSSION

1. "Life is not worth living, apart from redemption." This is how Oswald Chambers identifies the theme of Ecclesiastes.[2] What has this passage revealed about man's salvation from the predicament of hopelessness? Compare Chambers' statement with 1 Corinthians 15:19.

2. Think more about the following subjects which appeared in the passage of this lesson:

(a) people's need of comfort (cf. Ps 119:81-83; Is 40:1-2; 51:3; Ps 23:4)

1. Robert Laurin, "Ecclesiastes," in *The Wycliffe Bible Commentary*, p. 590.
2. Oswald Chambers, *Shade of His Hand*, preface.

Do you try to comfort others in their distresses?
(*b*) resurrection of the body
> for believers, glory (1 Co 15:20-22; Jn 5:29)
> for unbelievers, judgment (Rev 20:11-13)

Can you visualize having a resurrected body in heaven?
(*c*) Is God both transcendent and immanent? Definitions:
> transcendent: above and beyond (Ec 5:2)
> immanent: within and around (Eph 4:6)

How does God relate to you in both attributes?
(*d*) true worship of God (Jn 4:24)
Is God worshiped only in a Sunday worship service?
3. What are some conditions for genuine enjoyment in the experience of a Christian? Consider these observations of one writer:

> The good things of the world are God's gifts to be enjoyed by us with thankfulness and contentment. [Cf. 1 Ti 4:4.]

> The key to enjoyment is to substitute grace for grab.

> The art of enjoyment usually comes readiest to those least cumbered with worldly goods.[3]

V. FURTHER STUDY

You may want to make a full study of the subject of joy and rejoicing in the Bible. An exhaustive concordance will help you to begin this topical study.[4]

VI. WORDS TO PONDER

Jesus' answer to man's pessimism and fatalism:

> Ask, and it shall be given you;
> seek, and ye shall find;
> knock, and it shall be opened unto you (Lk 11:9).

3. G. S. Hendry, "Ecclesiastes," in *The New Bible Commentary*, p. 542.
4. Two recommended concordances are James Strong, *The Exhaustive Concordance to The Bible*; and Robert Young, *Analytical Concordance to the Bible*.

Third Sermon:
Who Knows What Is Good?

ECCLESIASTES ALWAYS HAS AN ANSWER

TO THE UNBELIEVING SKEPTIC WHO IS

OVERWHELMED BY THE FUTILITY OF LIFE.

In the passage of this lesson the skeptic blasts, "Who knows what is good for man in this life?" (6:12). The preacher's answer is simple and sure, "The truly wise man knows" (8:5).

In Lesson 1 we observed that Ecclesiastes is classified with Proverbs and Job as wisdom literature. This is because so much is written about wisdom in these books. In Ecclesiastes the word *wise* appears twenty-five times, and the word *wisdom*, twenty-eight times. The largest concentration of these words is in chapter 7 of this third sermon. An important part of our study will focus on the meaning and outworking of this true wisdom, which is a key to the preacher's message.

I. PREPARATION FOR STUDY

1. Read Proverbs 1:7 and note where true wisdom begins in a person's experience. A study of *wisdom* and its cognates in Proverbs reveals that the wise man is he who trusts in the Lord for his salvation, is accounted righteous in His sight, and who walks in personal fellowship with Him. Obviously this kind of wisdom is not mere head knowledge. It is the spiritual life and character of one who has experienced the saving work of God in his whole being. You will want to keep this in mind as you study the passage of this lesson.

2. Review survey Chart D, observing the two parts of this third sermon.

II. ANALYSIS

Segment to be analyzed: 6:1—8:13
Paragraph divisions: at verses 6:1, 7, 10; 7:1, 11, 15, 19, 23; 8:1, 10. Mark these in your Bible.

A. General Analysis

1. Read the entire segment for overall impressions. Does there seem to be a logical progression of thought from paragraph to paragraph, or is this hard to detect?
2. If you have not done so in an earlier lesson, underline or circle every appearance of the familiar words *vanity*, and *under the sun*, and *God*.
3. Read the passage once again paragraph by paragraph, and record a paragraph title in each of the oblique spaces of Chart G (examples given).

THIRD SERMON:
Who Knows What Is Good? (6:1—8:13)

Chart G

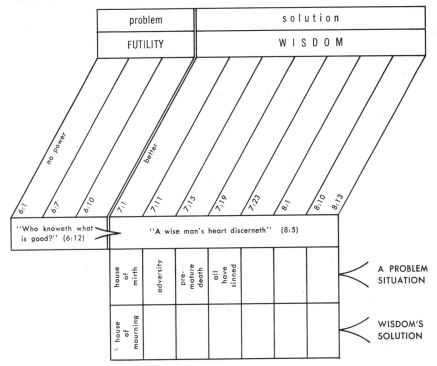

4. Read in your Bible the question of 6:12 which is recorded on Chart G. Then read the answer of 8:5. (Note: the word *discerneth* in the King James Version translates the same Hebrew word as *knoweth* in 6:12.)

5. Observe that this sermon follows the general pattern of the earlier two: the preacher first speaks about the problem of futility (ch. 6); then he gives the solution (7:1—8:13).

6. Note on the bottom of the chart the two unfinished topical studies, identified as *a problem situation* and *wisdom's solution*. More will be said about these later.

7. Underline in your Bible the various appearances of the words *wise* and *wisdom* in 7:1—8:13. Note that the last paragraph makes no references to these words. Some Bible students see this paragraph as the beginning of a new unit of thought. We will be studying it as the concluding paragraph of the third sermon.

B. Paragraph Analysis

PARAGRAPHS 6:1-6, 7-9, 10-12: Futility

1. Read the three paragraphs carefully, and record below what the preacher sees as futile in each paragraph. (See *Notes* on verses 4, 5, 10.)

6:1-6 _____

_____

6:7-9 _____

_____

6:10-12 _____

_____

2. Compare the words *appetite* (6:7) and *desire* (6:9). These words represent the main theme of paragraph 6:7-9.

3. Which of the following words best describes the tone of the third paragraph: cynical, bitter, doubting, inquiring?

PARAGRAPHS 7:1-10, 11-14, 15-18, 19-22, 23-29; 8:1-9, 10-13: Wisdom

The thing to keep in mind as you study these seven paragraphs is that the skeptic, speaking in all of chapter 6, has been asking one basic question: "Is it humanly possible for someone to know what is good?" (6:12). The answer of the seven paragraphs is that it is possible, for the person who is truly wise—he who trusts in God with all his heart and hears His voice in a personal way.

Refer to Chart G and recall that you had observed the unfinished topical studies at the bottom of the chart. Now is the time to complete these studies. As you read each of the seven paragraphs, record a word or phrase which identifies the problem situation, and also record what solution wisdom has to offer. Examples are given. Keep in mind what is meant by this wisdom, as discussed earlier in the lesson. In the last paragraph the wise man is the God-fearing man. (Note: Sometimes more than one answer is possible for each blank space. You may want to record your own answers even for the paragraphs where examples are supplied.)

Many other things are said about wisdom in these paragraphs. Record these on a piece of paper as you move from paragraph to paragraph.

Below are a few selected questions and suggestions concerning the text of this section.

Paragraph 7:1-10. Compare the question of 6:12 "What is good?" with the opening phrase of 7:1: "A good name."

_____

_____

In what sense is the "day of death" better than "the day of one's birth" (7:1)? Compare verse 8. _____

_____

Is the preacher here censoring laughter and pure pleasure? What is his point? _____

Paragraph 7:11-14. How does wisdom compare with money, according to verse 12? _____

_____

Paragraph 7:15-18. Do you think verses 16-17 intend to discourage the believer from a pursuit of godliness, in view of the total teaching of Scripture (e.g. 1 Timothy 4:7; 6:11)? If not, what is the point here? (See *Notes.*) _____

_____

Paragraph 7:19-22. Read verses 19-20 using these paraphrases: "Righteousness strengtheneth the righteous" (v. 19). "There is not a righteous man upon earth, that . . . sinneth not" (v. 20).

Compare verse 20 with Romans 3:23. _____

_____

Does verse 20 contradict verse 19? In what sense is a believer righteous, even though he commits sins from time

to leave (cf. Ro 3:21-22; 4:3, 5)? _____

_____

Paragraph 7:23-29. This paragraph describes the preacher's search mission: "I applied mine heart . . . to search" (7:25). What could he not find? What did he find? Record the latter:

"I find" (7:26) _____

"I found" (7:28) _____

"this only have I found" (7:29) _____

Paragraph 8:1-9. Verse 1 extols the wise man, and the remainder of the paragraph describes how the wise citizen respects the authority of government. Verse 2 is the key verse of this paragraph. What should be the basic motive

in obeying the laws of one's country? _____

_____

Read this paragraph in a paraphrase version such as the Living Bible to catch the meaning of unclear parts of the text.

Paragraph 8:10-13. Although the words *wise* and *wisdom* do not appear here, the reference to "them that fear God" (v. 12) is to wise men.

According to 8:10-12a, justice does not seem to triumph.

How is this misconception corrected by verse 13? _____

_____

In what sense shall it "be well with them that fear God"

(8:12)? _____

_____

Note the strength of the next phrase: "which fear before him," that is, which *openly* fear him.

III. NOTES

1. "For he cometh in with vanity" (6:4). *He* may be translated "it," referring to the miscarriage of 6:3b. See the New American Standard Bible for a translation of verses 4-5.

2. "Do not all go to one place?" (6:6). In Old Testament times, the spirits of all the deceased went to the one place, Sheol. But there were two regions of Sheol: a place of torment for unbelievers (Ps 9:17; Deu 32:22), and a place of rest and bliss for believers (cf. Ps 16:10; Job 3:11-19). Today, the spirits of unbelievers go to Hades (Lk 16:23-25) to await in agony the appearance before the great white throne judgment; and the spirits of believers go to paradise, in the presence of Christ (cf. Lk 23:43).[1]

3. "The living will lay it to his heart" (7:2). New American Standard Bible reads, "The living takes it to heart."

4. "By the sadness of the countenance the heart is made better" (7:3). The Berkeley Version footnote comments, "A good cry relieves emotional upheaval."

5. "God also hath set the one over against the other" (7:14). *The Living Bible* paraphrases the last half of 7:14 thus: "God gives one as well as the other—so that everyone will realize that nothing is certain in this life."

6. "Be not righteous over much" (7:16). Leupold interprets this as an overstrained righteousness which grows out of conceit.[2] There is also a false sophisticated wisdom ("neither make thyself over wise") such as the Pharisees displayed in their love to be called "Rabbi, Rabbi" (Mt 23:7).

IV. FOR THOUGHT AND DISCUSSION

1. How do you reconcile 6:2a (what God gives) and 6:2b (what God does not give)?

---

1. In the King James Old Testament the Hebrew word *sheol* is always translated "hell." This hell is not the place of eternal torment referred to in Revelation 20:10. In the King James New Testament, ten of the twenty-two appearances of the word *hell* translate the Greek *hades*. Again, this is not the eternal location of torment, but the transitional place of torment.
2. H. C. Leupold, *Exposition of Ecclesiastes*, p. 164.

2. What is the truer measurement of a man's character: what he sets out to do, or what he actually gets done (see 7:8)?

3. How would you describe a righteous, holy life?

4. Do you think a Christian's countenance should reflect something of his being a redeemed child of God (see 8:1)?

5. Should you as a Christian citizen obey all the laws of your country? Read Matthew 22:21; Romans 13:1-7; 1 Peter 2:13-17. Suppose you do not agree with some of those laws? Should a believer deny his Lord if commanded to do so by a secular ruler? In such a case is the ruler staying within his boundaries of "the things which are Caesar's" (Mt 22:21)?

6. Do the scales of divine justice always settle and balance quickly? If not, why the delays?

V. FURTHER STUDY

Make a topical study in the Bible of things that are good. Begin by deciding on a solid definition of "good."

VI. WORDS TO PONDER

I found that though God has made men upright, each has turned away to follow his own downward road (7:29, TLB).

Fourth Sermon:
Remember Now Thy Creator

THIS FOURTH SERMON IS THE PREACHER'S

FINAL ANALYSIS OF THE PROBLEM OF

LIFE'S FUTILITY AND ITS ONLY SOLUTION.

He recognizes that the problem is complex, and even mysterious, because life is made up of so many paradoxes. But he is wise to see that the answer is simple: Trust God, *regardless*. "Remember now thy Creator" (12:1) is the last exhortation of the sermon, a clear instruction on how faith will drive away the dark clouds of futility.

I. PREPARATION FOR STUDY

Review Chart D again, to see the context of the passage of this lesson.

II. ANALYSIS

Segment to be analyzed: 8:14—12:7
Paragraph divisions: at verses 8:14, 16; 9:1, 4, 11, 13; 10:1; 11:1, 7; 12:1. Mark these in your Bible.

A. General Analysis

1. Read the entire passage through once for overall impressions. Observe how chapters 10-11 sound like the book of Proverbs. (Note: the reason for not including 12:8 in this segment will be discussed in the next lesson.)
2. Read again 8:14—9:18, paragraph by paragraph. What aspect of futility appears in each paragraph? Record your observations in the oblique spaces of Chart H. (An example is given.)

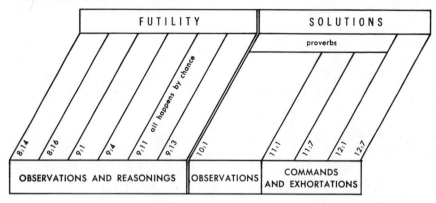

3. Observe on Chart H how this fourth sermon follows the same general pattern as the other three: first, observations of the futility of life; and second, solutions to the problem of futility.

B. Paragraph Analysis

PARAGRAPHS 8:14—9:18. Futility
Only a few selected questions on these six paragraphs are given here.

1. How is 8:15 the unbeliever's reaction to the futility of

8:14? _____ .

2. Why is man unable to discover and fathom all the works

of God (8:16-17)? _____

3. Read a modern paraphrase for a suggestion as to what 9:1b means.

4. The familiar maxim says, "Where there's life, there's

hope." How does 9:4-10 illustrate this? _____

_____

The skeptic, through the mouth of the preacher, has been charging all along that life is futile. Is he now conceding

some value to life? In effect, what is he saying? _____

_____

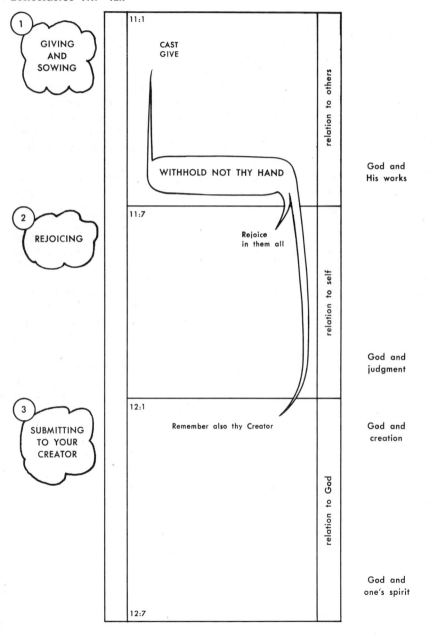

5. Two good acts are cited in 9:15: deliverance of a city, and recognition of the deliverer. Which one was not performed? Why is so much made of such ingratitude? _____

PARAGRAPH 10:1-20. Proverbs
At chapter 10 the preacher begins to describe the large view of life—the true view—which can be the only answer to the frustrated skeptic. In 8:14—9:18 the skeptic recognized the existence of two groups of people—righteous and evil (9:2)—but he measured them only by apparent consequences: for example, one fate common to all (9:2-3). The error of such a view is in its reaching sweeping conclusions from generalities. So in chapter 10 the preacher cites specific details of the lives of wise men and evil men, and shows that the profitable and successful life is that of the wise man. Read this chapter and record on paper some of the descriptions and consequences of the deeds of the wise man and of the fool.

PARAGRAPHS 11:1—12:7. Commands and Exhortations
Observe on Chart H that most of chapter 10 is a listing of observations—in the style of Proverbs—about wisdom and folly. The remainder of the sermon (11:1—12:7) revolves around exhortations and commands, appealing for a consecrated walk in the knowledge and fear of God.
Chart I is a partially completed analytical chart of the segment 11:1—12:7.[1] Use this as a worksheet to record other key words, phrases, and outlines as you proceed with your study of the text.
1. Read 11:1-6. Note that the phrase "withhold not thine hand" (v. 6) is the key phrase of Chart I. (See *Notes* on this phrase.) What are some of the teachings of this paragraph about not holding back? _____

What can we learn from nature about this subject? _____

How many times is the phrase "thou knowest not" re-

1. Detailed instructions on the analytical chart method are given in Irving L. Jensen, *Independent Bible Study.*

48

peated in the paragraph? How is it related to the thought

of not holding back, or not being idle? _____

What is the one reference to God in this paragraph? _____

_____

Observe on Chart I that this paragraph is primarily about one's relation to others. How are the other two paragraphs

identified? _____

_____

2. Read 11:7-10. What is the tone of this paragraph? _____

_____

How is this tone set in the very first phrase? _____

_____

Note the repetition of the word *rejoice* and similar words. Underline these in your Bible. Observe the two places where the reference to rejoicing is tempered by other factors.

Complete the following, from the Bible text:

(*a*) "If a man . . . rejoice . . . *yet* _____."
    (11:8)

(*b*) "Rejoice, O young man . . . *but* _____."
    (11:9)

Do you think the words which follow *yet* and *but* are warnings against rejoicing? Or do you think they are intended to enrich and purify the experience of rejoicing?

_____

Compare the readings of these verses in modern versions.

3. Read 12:1-7. This is the Bible's classic description of old age, written in the form of allegory. It is an appropriate conclusion to the message of the whole book of Ecclesiastes, before the epilogue of 12:8-14 appears. Follow carefully the study suggestions given below:

What are the *time* references in the opening verse (v. 1)

and closing verse (v. 7)? _____

As noted above, most of the pictures of this paragraph are allegorical, representing literal aspects of old age. For example, look at verse 3:

TEXT	MEANING
keepers of the house	hands and arms
strong men	legs
grinders	teeth
those that look out of the windows	eyes

Refer to a commentary for interpretations of the remaining allegories, or read the paraphrase of *The Living Bible.*
The first ten words of this paragraph are the key to its meaning and purpose. What do you think is meant here by the word *Remember*? _____

_____

Is this picture of old-age decay inevitable for all—that is, for the believer as well as the unbeliever? In view of your answer, what do you think is the purpose of the command of verse 1? _____

_____

Evaluate these two suggested purposes:
(*a*) Honor your Creator now, because when you get old it will be very hard to exert body, soul, and spirit in the zealous service of His kingdom.
(*b*) Put your trust in God now, because when you get old you probably will not have the desire to turn to Him. Observe how *The Living Bible* interprets the purpose of 12:1-2:

> Don't let the excitement of being young cause you to forget about your Creator. Honor him in your youth before the evil years come—when you'll no longer enjoy living. It will be too late then to try to remember him, when the sun and light and moon and stars are dim to your old eyes, and there is no silver lining left among your clouds.

Refer to Chart I again and reflect on the connection between the phrases "withhold not thy hand" and "remember thy Creator." Compare Romans 12:1 with this.

III. NOTES

1. "No man knoweth either hatred or love" (9:1). This may be paraphrased: No one knows whether God will give

favor or not. Such an interpretation is in line with the theme of the paragraph, that one fate comes to all.

2. "The dead know not any thing" (9:5). This verse does not support the doctrine of soul sleep. Archer says that it "simply means that the dead have no more knowledge of a personal future with its opportunities of choice for or against God, and between life and good, and death and evil, such as they had prior to the grave."[2]

3. "The words of wise men are heard in quiet" (9:17). *The Living Bible* paraphrases this: "The quiet words of a wise man are better."

4. "Yielding pacifieth great offenses" (10:4). That is, "Composure may remedy serious mistakes" (Berkeley).

5. Wisdom is profitable to direct" (10:10). New American Standard Bible reads, "Wisdom has the advantage of giving success."

6. "A babbler is no better" (10:11). The Berkeley Version gives the sense of the entire verse: "If the snake bites before the charming, then the charmer's skill does not benefit."

7. "But money answereth all things" (10:19). Read *but* as *and* (NASB). Then the three phrases of verse 19 are seen as a threefold description of profligate living.

8. "Withhold not thine hand" (11:6). A literal rendering is, "Do not let down your hand." New American Standard Bible translates, "Do not be idle."

9. "The spirit shall return unto God" (12:7). At death a man's body returns to dust (Gen 3:19), and his spirit is committed to God (cf. Ac 7:59), who sovereignly controls and determines his eternal destiny. At the end of time the dust will be reclothed in resurrection and joined with the man's spirit, whether for eternal glory or eternal damnation.

IV. FOR THOUGHT AND DISCUSSION

1. Have you observed in life some of the same paradoxes mentioned in 8:14—9:18? Are you disturbed by these?

2. Reflect on the significance of the phrase "man cannot find out" (8:17). Can man discover the truth through *reason*? Does this explain why God has given *revelation* to man? Would you know how to be saved if God had not revealed the way to you?

2. Gleason L. Archer, *A Survey of Old Testament Introduction*, p. 471.

3. Does a person have a second chance to be saved, *after* he has died? How does this magnify the critical nature of the breath of life? Read 9:4a with this in mind.

4. "Time and chance happeneth to them all" (9:11). Do you agree?

5. Why should Christians, of all people, live full lives of outgoing service and liberal giving? Besides Romans 12:1, what other New Testament verses remind you of the phrase "withhold not thine hand" (Ec 11:6)?

6. "If you wait for perfect conditions, you will never get anything done." (This is how *The Living Bible* applies Ecclesiastes 11:4.) Have you ever postponed doing something until you could do it perfectly? Who actually accomplishes more: the perfectionist (idealist), or the practical man (pragmatist)? How should a Christian deal with sins and imperfections in the performance of his Christian duties?

7. Compare Philippians 4:4 and Ecclesiastes 11:8a. Give some reasons why Christian living should be joyful living. What is your definition of joy?

8. What about zeal and enthusiasm in the Christian's life? Why is it so important to be a zealous believer as a young person? Do you think any blessings carry over from youth into one's later years? Does a Christian need to dread the physical and mental limitations of old age?

9. It is an accepted fact that the best time to give one's heart to Christ is in childhood or youth. Cite some reasons why this is so.

V. FURTHER STUDY

For New Testament studies on how to live as a young Christian and how to triumph as an aged saint, read Paul's two letters to Timothy. Timothy is the youth, and Paul is the old man.

VI. WORDS TO PONDER

Keep on sowing your seed, for you never know which will grow—perhaps it all will (11:6, TLB).

The Conclusion of the Whole Matter

THE EPILOGUE OF ECCLESIASTES IS

A CONDENSED SUMMARY OF ALL THAT THE

PREACHER HAS TAUGHT IN HIS SERMONS.

Recall that each of his sermons was of two parts: the first recognizing the frustration of futility, and the second offering solutions to this problem. So it does not surprise us to find both of these subjects reappearing in the epilogue. Many who study Ecclesiastes and finally arrive at the verse 12:8—called by one writer "the dust-heap of *vanitas vanitatum*"—are disappointed or confused because they feel the writer has returned full-circle back to his bleak starting point in 1:2, "Vanity of vanities." By studying 12:8 in the context of 12:9-14, however, we will see the appearance of that verse at the end of the book to be a very natural one.

I. PREPARATION FOR STUDY

1. Review the survey Chart D, observing how the epilogue concludes the book of Ecclesiastes.
2. Read 1:14, and recall that when the preacher says that all is vanity, he means all that which man sees from his limited, sinful viewpoint, from under the sun. The very fact of a higher, enlightened viewpoint, furnished by revelation of God, suggests there is a solution to man's frustration of futility, and this gospel of solution is what the preacher has been trying to share with his hearers and readers in each of his sermons.

II. ANALYSIS

Segment to be analyzed: 12:8-14

Paragraph divisions: at verses 8, 9, 11, 13. Mark these in your Bible.

1. Read the segment once. Which paragraphs record the words of the preacher? Which paragraph is about the preacher himself?

SUMMARY EPILOGUE (12:8-14)

Chart J

FUTILITY	SOURCE OF SOLUTION		SOLUTION
PROBLEM restated	"Moreover, because the preacher was wise, he still taught" 12:9a. MINISTRY OF GOD'S WORD		CONCLUSION
12:8	12:9	12:11	12:13 12:14
All is vanity	good acceptable (delightful) correct true	stimulating (goads) secure (nails) divine final	Fear God

2. Chart J is a work sheet which shows the thought structure of this epilogue. Record other words and phrases on the chart as you proceed with your study.

3. Observe on the chart the first and last sections, called *futility* and *solution*. These are the two familiar parts of the former sermons which we have been studying. What section on the chart is located between these two? Does this sound like a logical location for it?

4. Note how the paraphrase of 12:9a, shown on the chart, is a contrast to the problem of vanity. Read 12:9-12 and observe every reference to God's Word, whether given by instruction of the preacher, or otherwise. Compare your observations with the lists shown on the chart.

5. What man sees (from under the sun) is not enough. God shows what man cannot see. This is revelation. Does this help to explain why God's revelation via His Word is the source for solving man's frustrations about the futility of life?

6. Compare the phrases "one shepherd" (v. 11) and "many books" (v. 12). Who is the "one shepherd"? _____ Has anyone spoken words as God has? Have many opinions ("many books") been expressed by men, over the centuries, as to where to find answers to life's problems? Whose answers must be correct: God's or man's? Where did the preacher find the words which he wrote in this book of Ecclesiastes (12:10)? _____

_____

7. Analyze carefully each word of the last paragraph. Note that Solomon clearly identifies this paragraph as the conclusion of the whole subject which he has undertaken in the book. In what ways is the truth of these verses the solution to the problem of 12:8? Reflect long on this before you answer. _____

_____

8. Record what is taught in 12:13-14 about each of the following subjects:

(a) God: His nature, and His works _____

_____

(*b*) sin and its judgment _____

_____

(*c*) man _____

_____

(*d*) way of salvation _____

_____

(*e*) final judgments _____

_____

(*f*) immortality of the soul _____

_____

9. Ponder more about the words "Fear God, and keep his commandments" (12:13). What are the two commands of this verse? How are they related to each other? Look at the two commands more closely to see if a redemptive aspect is involved.

"Fear God." What do you think is meant by the word fear here? (See 2 Timothy 1:7 for a different meaning.) Do you think love, honor, and reverence are involved? For help in answering this, read the following passages where the word appears: Deuteronomy 6:1-9; 8:6-7; 10:12-13; 31:12-13; Psalm 25:14; Proverbs 1:7; 14:27; Romans 3:18; 2 Corinthians 7:1; Hebrews 11:7; 12:28; 1 Peter 2:17. Note that all the references to God in the Deuteronomy passages are "the Lord your God." Such a faith is not mere acknowledgment of God as Creator, but trust in Him as Saviour (the connotation of *Jehovah* in the Old Testament). Why do you think Ecclesiastes 12:13 reads "Fear God" rather than "Fear the Lord thy God"? (Recall that the word *Lord* does not appear at all in Ecclesiastes.) Is the preacher trying to get his reader to first come to a place of faith and trust in God as Creator, from natural revelation, so that he then will respond to whatever special revelation God gives him and trust in Him as his personal Lord? "Keep his commandments." This is a common phrase throughout the Old Testament. It cannot teach salvation by works, for this contradicts the clear teaching of the Bible (e.g. Eph 2:9; Ps 51:16-17). A saving faith is always the basis for acceptable works. A person who is saved has put his trust in God and in this new relationship wants to live in obedience to His Word ("keep his commandments"). This is the teaching of the New Testament as well as the Old Testament (e.g. "faith without works is dead," Ja 2:20; "faith wrought with his works," Ja 2:21).

In view of the remainder of the paragraph (12:13b-14), it seems that the phrase "keep his commandments" is meant for those who have come to a personal relationship of trust in God as his Saviour. But even a believer knows he cannot perfectly keep God's commandments. Does this jeopardize his salvation? No. Such a conviction should deepen his trust in God, for he must therefore rely wholly on the mercy and grace of God not to cast him off. And God does *not* reject him, because the sins are atoned for by Christ's death. God sees Christ's righteousness when He looks upon the heart of the man who truly fears Him. This is the ultimate basis of all Old Testament verses which teach the way of salvation. The further revelation of the New Testament completes the story of redemption as it is to be found in Christ (Heb 1:1-3). Bringing the Old and New Testaments together by way of example, it is correct to say that Christ's blood atoned for the sins of Abraham, for "Abraham believed God, and it was imputed unto him for righteousness" (Ja 2:23).

10. Read 12:14. This last verse of Ecclesiastes reaches to the end of time, when the holy God must "bring every work into judgment." Would such an awesome verse be connected to verse 13 if the latter were not referring to a person's spiritual salvation? Read Revelation 20:12-13, which teaches the final judgment of all unbelievers. The sins of believers were judged at the cross of Christ, but there will be a judgment of the works of their lives after the rapture of the church. For this, read Romans 14:10 and 2 Corinthians 5:10.

11. Note that the last verse of Ecclesiastes refers to the ultimate manifestation of good and righteousness, as well as to the judgment of evil. Over and over again in the book of Ecclesiastes, injustice is what the observer sees under the sun. God's answer is that every event of all time is weighed on the scales of His justice and holiness.

III. NOTES

1. "Acceptable words" (12:10). The word *acceptable* means "delightful (NASB); "pleasing" (RSV).

2. "Upright" (12:10). The Berkeley Version translates the last line of 12:10 as, "to write correctly the reliable words of truth." All Bible authors wrote with the intention of accuracy; only the Holy Spirit could override human frailty and guarantee infallibility of their writing.

3. "Goads" (12:11). A goad was a farmer's long wooden pole, having a spade at one end for removing mud from his plow, and a sharp spur at the other end for prodding his oxen. Recall the words of the Lord to Paul, "It is hard for thee to kick against the pricks" (Ac 9:5).

4. "One shepherd" (12:11). This is the one Shepherd, the Lord himself.

IV. FOR THOUGHT AND DISCUSSION

1. "God . . . hath in these last days spoken unto us by his Son" (Heb 1:1-2). What has the Father said about His Son? Has He commanded man to believe on Him if he is to be saved?

2. How is Jesus, as the living Word, God's answer to the complaint of man about the futility of life?

3. What do you think is the connection between faith and works in the life of a Christian?

4. Would there be eternal hope for a sinner if Christ had not died in his place?

5. What important truths have you learned from the passage of this lesson? Do you "fear God, and keep his commandments"?

*   *   *

A Concluding Thought

All the books of the Old Testament point to the coming of the King and Saviour, Jesus Christ. Ecclesiastes is no exception, for it leads those living under the sun to the Son. There is only one escape route from the darkness of this world to the light of God's heaven. That is Jesus Himself, who said, "I am the way, the truth, and the life: no man cometh unto the Father, but by me" (Jn 14:6).

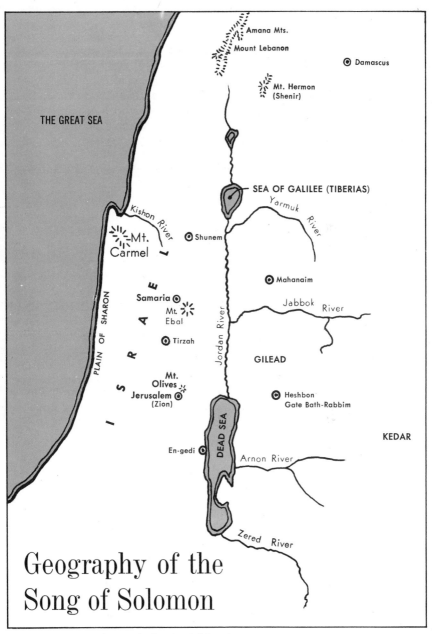

Geography of the Song of Solomon

(Note: The locations of Baal-hamon [8:11] and **Bether** [2:17] are unknown. Bether may not be a proper name [see Berkeley Version].)

Song of Solomon: Background and Survey

A HEALTHY BALANCE IN BIBLE STUDY

IS MAINTAINED WHEN THE SONG OF SOLOMON

IS STUDIED ALONG WITH ECCLESIASTES.

Ecclesiastes focuses on the intellect of man—his mental outlook on life. The Song of Solomon is a book about the emotions of man—in particular, the emotion of love.

It is recognized that man's total experience is directed by these three responses: intellect, emotions, and will. Actually all three responses are involved in a full experience of genuine love, just as this is true of genuine faith. To say that the Song of Solomon is a book about the emotion of love is not to rule out intellect and will.[1] It is just that the emotion aspect is prominent in the story.

But the Song of Solomon is more than a human love story. It is a picture of the love between God and His people. If your study of the Song of Solomon will arouse in you a more genuine love for your Lord as well as a deeper gratitude for His love to you, then it will not surprise you that God chose to include such a love story in His holy Scriptures.

I. BACKGROUND

(Note: Because of the length of this lesson, you may want to study it in three separate units: first background; then survey; then a literal interpretation of the whole book. The last-named project appears at the close of this lesson.)

A. Title

The opening verse gives the title "The song of songs." This is the Hebrew way of expressing the superlative. Of Sol-

---

1. For example, a person in love exercises his will in choosing whom to love.

omon's 1005 songs (1 Ki 4:32), this one was his best and most important. The more common title assigned to the book is *Song of Solomon,* also based on 1:1. Sometimes the book is referred to as *Canticles* (series of songs).

B. Author

The traditional view is that Solomon was the author. This is strongly supported by internal characteristics of the book. (Refer to outside sources for a discussion of this.) The name Solomon appears at these places in the book: 1:1, 5; 3:7, 9, 11; 8:11, 12. The reference at 1:1 may be translated either "of Solomon" or "about Solomon."

C. Date Written

Solomon probably wrote this while he was still young, before being drawn away from Jehovah by his seven hundred wives (1 Ki 11:3-4). A suggested date is 965 B.C.

D. Relation to Other Books of the Bible

In our English Bibles the Song of Solomon is the fifth of the poetical books, following Job, Psalms, Proverbs, and Ecclesiastes. In the Hebrew Bible it is the first of the Five Rolls (*Megilloth*): Song of Solomon, Ruth, Lamentations, Ecclesiastes, Esther. Portions of it were sung on the eighth day of the Passover feast, which was the Jews' first and greatest of the annual feasts. In ancient times the Jews revered Canticles as uniquely sublime. They likened Proverbs to the outer court of the temple; Ecclesiastes to the holy place; and Song of Solomon to the most holy place. The New Testament book which has the same type of purpose as the Song of Solomon—reflection about Christ and His church—is the epistle to the Ephesians.

E. Form

The book is a unified lyrical poem. It is a series of stanzas or songs of varied lengths.[2] Our later survey study will

2. The New Scofield Reference Bible divides the text into these thirteen canticles (songs):
    I.   1:2-6 A Young Bride, a Shulamite Girl
   II.   1:7-8 The Perplexed Bride
  III.   1:9-17 Mutual Admiration
  IV.   2:1-7 The Shulamite Is Comforted
   V.   2:8-17 The Shulamite Describes a Happy Visit

reveal that there is a topical unity of the various songs, even though there is no defined dramatical progression, as in the book of Job. Because of its poetical form, we may expect to find the usual figures of speech found in poetry (e.g. metaphor: "thy hair is as a flock of goats," 4:1). Also, the phraseology of the poetry is strictly oriental and must be read in that light (e.g. chap. 4).

F. Setting of the Story

The main characters of the Song of Solomon are Solomon, a Shulamite woman, and a group called "daughters of Jerusalem."

1. Solomon—king of Israel (1 Ki 1:32-37), son of David and Bathsheba (2 Sa 12:24).

2. Shulamite woman—The name *Shulamite* appears only at 6:13. It is probably derived from the place Shunem, located a short distance north of Jezreel near the plain of Megiddo (cf. Jos 19:18; 1 Sa 28:4; 1 Ki 1:3; 2 Ki 4:8). See the map on page 59.

3. Daughters of Jerusalem—The identity of these women is not disclosed. They may have been companions of the bride, attendants of the king's palace, or interested onlookers.

Some commentators assign a few verses of the text to other speakers (e.g. an officer of the king's guard, 3:7-10).

H. A. Ironside's description of the setting of this story, as summarized by Merrill Unger, is quoted here at length.

King Solomon had a vineyard in the hill country of Ephraim, about 50 miles N of Jerusalem, 8:11. He let it out to keepers, 8:11, consisting of a mother, two sons, 1:6, and two daughters— the Shulamite, 6:13, and a little sister, 8:8. The Shulamite was "the Cinderella" of the family, 1:5, naturally beautiful but unnoticed. Her brothers were likely half brothers, 1:6. They made her work very hard tending the vineyards, so that she had little opportunity to care for her personal appearance, 1:6. She pruned the vines and set traps for the little foxes, 2:15. She also kept the flocks, 1:8. Being out in the open so much, she became sunburned, 1:5.

One day a handsome stranger came to the vineyard. It was Solomon disguised. He showed an interest in her, and she became embarrassed concerning her personal appearance, 1:6. She took him for a shepherd and asked about his flocks, 1:7. He answered evasively, 1:8, but also spoke loving words to her, 1:8-10, and promised rich gifts for the future, 1:11. He won her heart and left with the promise that some day he would return. She dreamed of him at night and sometimes thought he was near, 3:1. Finally he did return in all his kingly splendor to make her his bride, 3:6-7.[3]

The above description will help you catch something of the tone of the book as you begin your study.

G. Schools of Interpretation

The Song of Solomon has been interpreted in three different ways:

1. Naturalistic—a human love story, of literary merit, with no typical or figurative meaning intended.

2. Allegorical—purely figurative, not based on historical fact.

3. Typical—teaching by example, from historical facts; and by type, from viewing these historical facts as figurative representations. In the words of Scroggie, "As in Jonah, we have allegory emerging from history."[4] G. Campbell Morgan describes this methodology of interpretation thus:

> The songs should be treated then, first as simple and yet sublime songs of human affection. When they are thus understood, reverently the thoughts may be lifted into the higher value of setting forth the joys of the communion between the spirit of man and the Spirit of God, and ultimately between the Church and Christ.[5]

This manual follows the typical view.

H. Typical Teaching

As indicated earlier, the characters of the dialogue of Canticles are Solomon, the Shulamite woman, and daughters of Jerusalem. In the story Solomon is the bridegroom, and the Shulamite woman is the bride.[6] Two applications of typical teaching may be intended here:

3. H. A. Ironside, *Addresses on The Song of Solomon*, pp. 17-21, summarized by Unger, *Unger's Bible Handbook*, pp. 299-300.
4. W. Graham Scroggie, *Know Your Bible*, 1:118.
5. G. Campbell Morgan, *The Analyzed Bible* (Westwood, N.J.: Revell, 1964), p. 197.
6. A figurative interpretation of the daughters of Jerusalem, if intended, might be that these are not saved ones, though near the kingdom of God.

1. Israel is the bride, and God is the bridegroom. Read these other Old Testament passages where this bride-and-groom relationship is clearly taught: Jer 2:2; Ho 2:16,[7] 18-20; Eze 16:8-14;[8] Is 54:5-6. Jewish believers of Old Testament times clearly saw this typical intent of Canticles, which helped to impress them as to the book's canonicity.

2. The church is the bride, and Christ the bridegroom. Read Eph 5:23-25; 2 Co 11:1-2; Rev 19:7-9; 21:9.

3. A third application is derived from the second, in the sense that an individual believer (of the whole believing church) is the particular object of Christ's love. From a practical standpoint, this is the most intimate application you can make of the book's typical teaching for your own Christian life.

Some Bible students see another character involved in the story of Canticles: a shepherd-lover (1:7), from whose affection Solomon tries to lure the Shulamite woman away:

> Solomon uses all the dazzle and splendor of his court to woo the girl away from her true love, seeking to get her to become one of his wives instead. In like manner the world is ever seeking to attract away from Christ those who are "espoused" to Him. Solomon is unable to accomplish his goal, however, for the Shulamite resists all his overtures and remains true to her beloved shepherd to whom, at last, she is reunited.[9]

The reason there are different views as to the plot of Canticles is that the speakers are not identified by name in the Bible text. For example, the two-speaker view (Solomon, Shulamite woman) says that Solomon speaks all of 4:1-15; whereas the three-speaker view says that Solomon is the speaker of 4:1-6, while 4:7-15 are the words of the shepherd-lover. As John Phillips points out, "the abiding value of the Song of Solomon is clear whichever view is taken. As human life finds its highest fulfillment in the love of man and woman, so spiritual life finds its highest fulfillment in the love of Christ and His Church."[10]

---

7. In the KJV *ishi* means "my husband," and *baali* means "my master."
8. Ezekiel 16:20-21, 32, 38 reveals the unfaithfulness of Israel to her husband, God.
9. See John Phillips, *Exploring the Scriptures* (Chicago: Moody, 1965), p. 116. One commentary which follows this view is Arthur E. Cundall, *Proverbs to Isaiah 39* (Grand Rapids: Eerdmans, 1968), pp. 50 ff.
10. John Phillips, *Exploring The Scriptures*, p. 116.

An interesting comparison has been made between Ecclesiastes and Song of Solomon involving their pointing to Christ:

> In Ecclesiastes we learn that without Christ we cannot be satisfied, even if we possess the whole world—the heart is too large for the object. In the Song of Solomon we learn that if we turn from the world and set our affections on Christ, we cannot fathom the infinite preciousness of His love—the Object is too large for the heart.[11]

I. Purposes

The purposes of the Song of Solomon are:
1. literal: to honor pure human love and marriage
2. figurative: to show the Lord's love for Israel, and Christ's love for His church and for each individual Christian; and how the bride in each case should return that love.

The literal purpose of the book has often been twisted by those not prepared to read frank and intimate expressions of love. Asceticism and lust—two perversions of the holiness of marriage—are slain by the message of this book. If the reader is licentiously excited when he reads the Song of Solomon, he is out of tune with its purpose. The literal message of the book is perverted only by those who do not see the purity and true beauty of all of God's creative acts.

J. Key to the Book

The key to the full meaning and purpose of the Song of Solomon is Jesus Christ. This is true of all the books of the Bible. The book as a love story is unexcelled only if Christ is the lover in its pages—for no one can surpass His love: "Christ liveth in me: and the life which I now live in the flesh I live by the faith of *the Son of God, who loved me, and gave himself for me*" (Gal 2:20, italics added). In the Song of Solomon it is the person of Christ, not His work, which is the prominent characteristic. ("He is altogether lovely," 5:16.) The Christian reader who involves himself in the book is sure to be overwhelmed by the beautiful and reassuring truth of his union and communion with such a Saviour.

11. Quoted by Robert Lee, *The Outlined Bible* (Westwood, N.J.: Revell, n.d.), p. 21.

K. Unique Characteristics

The Song of Solomon is unique among the books of the Bible in many ways. Some of these are described below.

1. It is one of the most misunderstood books of the Bible. Its oriental expressions of intimate love partly account for this.

2. It is the only book of the Bible where love between humans is the main plot and theme. (Similar passages of love are to be found in Psalm 45 and the book of Ruth.)

3. There is only one reference to God in the book ("the Lord," 8:6 NASB). In the King James Version there is no reference. Instead, at 8:6 the Hebrew word *Yah* is translated "vehement."

4. There is no specific or direct reference to sin.

5. There is no specific or direct reference to the religious realm as such.

6. No other Old Testament book is alluded to here.

7. The book is not alluded to by Christ, nor is it quoted elsewhere in the New Testament.

8. The historicity of the book's action is clear. One support of this is its geographical setting—there are over fifteen geographical references. (See map on p. 59.)

L. Applying the Book

This book was written especially to stir the feelings of God's people. Ecclesiastes stresses thinking; the Song of Solomon stresses feeling, of the meditative type. Andrew Miller wrote long ago, "There is nothing which the men of this world dread more than solitude and reflection. They would rather be overpressed with engagements than have leisure for thought."[12] Human nature has not changed since! The Christological purpose of Canticles is to inspire Christians to take time to meditate on Jesus Christ. "The calm, reflective quiet of the soul in communion with the Person of the the exalted Lord, is what characterises its sweetest moments while here on earth."[13] The experience of Jonathan Edwards in reading the book was that from time to time an increased sweetness would carry him away in his contemplations. As you prepare to study the text of this important book of the Bible, ask God to open the eyes

12. Andrew Miller, *Meditations on The Song of Solomon* (London: Wheeler, n.d.), p. 1.
13. *Ibid.*

of your soul and to warm your heart as you meditate on Christ your Saviour and Lord. This is the supreme application of the Song of Solomon to your life.

II. SURVEY

The purpose of survey is to view the Song of Solomon in a general way and thus to discover its main theme. Here we will not dwell on details nor pursue interpretations.

A. A First Reading

Because the parts of the dialogue of these poems are not identified in the Bible text as to who is speaking, it is important to mark your Bible showing who the speakers are, if your Bible does not already show this in its headings.[14] The speakers shown below begin each new part at the verses cited. Mark these in your Bible.[15]

The Shulamite woman: 1:2, 4b, 5, 12, 16; 2:3; 4:16; 5:2, 10; 6:2; 7:9b; 8:10, 14

Solomon: 1:8, 15; 2:2; 4:1; 5:1a; 6:4, 13b; 8:5b, 13

Daughters of Jerusalem: 1:4b, 11; 3:6; 5:9; 6:1, 13a; 8:5a, 8

Read through the Song of Solomon in one sitting, aloud if possible. What are your first impressions? What one word clearly expresses the main subject of this book?

B. A Survey Chart

The Song of Solomon is difficult to outline in detail, because a progressing plot is not detectable, except in a general way. Chart K will help you see the main parts of this book. You may base your later studies on it.

1. Note that Canticles has a title verse (1:1), but no formal conclusion such as we are accustomed to find in Bible books. Read 1:1, then read the last few verses of chapter 8.

---

14. Versions which identify the speakers include: New Scofield Reference Bible (King James Version); New American Standard Bible; Berkeley Version; and *The Living Bible* (paraphrase).
15. For a few of the parts it is difficult to determine who the speaker is (e.g. 6:11). This accounts for differences shown in the headings of commentaries and versions. The lessons of this manual will follow the dialogue as shown by the given references. For the most part these are the designations of the New American Standard Bible.

SONG OF SOLOMON   UNION AND COMMUNION

Chart K

CHIEF SPEAKERS

COURTSHIP DAYS — bride
WEDDING — groom
MARRIED LIFE — wife — husband — both

TITLE 1:1 1:2 2:8 3:6 5:2 6:4 8:5 8:14

"Tell me . . . . where thou feedest"
"Behold, he cometh!"

bride muses about her courtship days — the wedding — troubled dream of separation — mutual love of husband and wife — the seal of their love

LOVE FIRST EXPRESSED AND EXPERIENCED

LOVE TRIED AND TRIUMPHANT

KEY VERSES
2:16
6:3
8:6a

KEY WORDS
beloved
love
fair
come

HE
"How beautiful you are" 1:15
"Put me like a seal over your heart." 8:6

SHE
"Let us run together" 1:4
"Leaning on her beloved" 8:5

QUEST

CONQUEST

68

2. Observe the six main segments shown on the chart, beginning at 1:2. Mark these major divisions in your Bible.

3. Study the outline shown directly under the main base line (beginning with "bride muses"). The heading *the wedding* is based partly on 3:11b (NASB), "the day of his wedding." Read 3:6-11. Scan the Bible text of the whole book again, segment by segment, and see if this outline represents the contents of each.

4. The top of the survey chart divides the Song of Solomon into three main parts. What are they? This general outline should be kept in mind throughout your analytical studies.

5. What outline on the chart divides the book into two main parts?

6. Note the progression from *quest* to *conquest*, involving bride and groom. Read the verses in your Bible. (Underline the verses in your Bible, as strong verses.)

7. Read the key verses which are cited on the chart. Be on the lookout for others as you study the book. Do the same for key words.

C. A Literal Interpretation of the Whole Book

No other book of the Bible gives such an extended description of the beauties of a love relationship between a man and a woman. The inclusion of this human love story in God's Book demonstrates the sacred honor which He has given to the union of husband and wife. Before moving on to the next lessons, where figurative interpretations are prominent, you may want to read the Song of Solomon first to learn its literal teachings about the kind of human love which honors God. Below is a partial list of aspects of love which you may expect to read about in the book.

PHYSICAL	
beauty	attraction
love	satisfaction
purity	giving and receiving
body	presence and separation
sexual instincts	physical wedlock
desire	

NON-PHYSICAL	
attraction	sacrifice
companionship	faithfulness
union and communion	praise
hope	beauty
pleasure	love
giving and receiving	purity
presence and separation	wholesomeness
tenderness	humility

For a concluding study, read the following New Testament passages for their teaching about:

(a) physical body: Ro 6:12-13, 19; 1 Co 6:18-20; 1 Th 5:23

(b) marriage: Mt 19:5-6; Eph 5:22-33; 1 Ti 4:1-5; 5:14; Heb 13:4; 1 Co 7

* * *

Some Review Questions

1. What does the title *Song of Songs* signify? What does the word *Canticles* mean?

2. Name and describe the three different views of interpretation of this book.

3. Who are the main characters of the book?

4. In the typical view of interpretation as applied to this church age, whom does Solomon represent? Whom does the Shulamite woman represent?

5. What are the purposes of this book as part of Scripture?

6. Name five unique characteristics of the book.

7. What are the three main divisions in the outline of Canticles?

8. Quote a key verse.

* * *

O Love Divine, how sweet Thou art!
When shall I find my willing heart
All taken up by Thee?
I thirst, I faint, I die to prove
The fulness of redeeming love,
The love of Christ to me.

CHARLES WESLEY

Seeking and Finding

AFTER A BRIEF TITLE VERSE,

THE INTIMATE SONGS OF LOVE

BEGIN TO SOUND THEIR MELODIES.

The reader acquainted with the other books of the Bible immediately senses that he has entered an entirely different chamber of the palace of Scripture. His first reaction may be that there is not much to be learned here of spiritual truth. And so he may hesitate to tarry, but the Holy Spirit invites him to stay on, for the love described in these pages of Scripture is pure and wholesome and God-glorifying. Beyond that, they portray the beautiful spiritual relationship between Christ and those whom He came to save.

I. PREPARATION FOR STUDY

1. Read again the setting of this story of Solomon and the Shulamite woman, as described in the early part of lesson 8. The poems of this lesson are some of the woman's reminiscences of her courtship days with Solomon. It is even possible that she may have been betrothed to him at this time, in a binding relationship prior to marriage:

> The Jewish law held espousal or engagement to be as binding as marriage . . . . After the betrothal, the groom could claim the bride at any time. The legal aspect of marriage was included in the betrothal; the wedding was merely a recognition of the agreement that had already been established.[1]

2. Keep in mind that the songs of this book are from an oriental culture. Many of the social customs and expressions of such a culture are foreign to the Western mind. Be

1. Merrill C. Tenney, "Luke," in *The Wycliffe Bible Commentary*, pp. 1030-31.

prepared to read expressions that are strange or unclear, and even appear too intimate for print. Read Titus 1:15; Philippians 4:8; and 2 Timothy 3:16-17 for a sound approach to a book like this.

3. Also keep in mind that there is not necessarily a rigid progression of plot from stanza to stanza in the dialogue of the passage. Do not feel frustrated as you study the Song of Solomon if there does not appear to be a continuity from one song to the next.

4. Read the title verse, 1:1. As indicated in lesson 8, the phrase *song of songs* means "the best song;" and the phrase *which is Solomon's* could also correctly translate the Hebrew as, "which is about Solomon."[2]

5. When you apply the story of this book to Christ and His relationship to you, remember that His love (*agape*) is perfect, complete, holy, and inexhaustible. At the most, an earthly story can only suggest and illustrate, in a limited manner, the glories of divine love.

II. ANALYSIS

Passage to be analyzed: 1:2—3:5

Stanza divisions: at verses 1:2, 4b, 5, 8, 11, 12, 15; 2:2, 3, 8, 10, 15; 3:1. Mark these in your Bible.

Use the accompanying work sheet (Chart L) to record any key words and phrases of the Bible text which you think are significant. Some are already recorded. The references move consecutively from top to bottom. The three columns clearly show the alternating pattern of dialogue.[3]

1. Keep referring to the work sheet as you study each stanza.

2. Who does most of the speaking in this passage? Observe the key outline of seeking and finding. Note how the dream of 3:1-4 brings both of these experiences together.

3. Can you think of a reason why paragraphs about mutual affection (1:8—2:7) are placed between the two sections

2. The Holy Spirit's ministry in the composition of the book is suggested by the answer to this question: How did Solomon, the author, learn the heart musings of the Shulamite woman?

3. As noted earlier, all of the dialogues of Canticles were not necessarily originally spoken in the sequence shown. However, there must be some designed purpose in the patterns in which they are recorded in the Bible text.

	Shulamite Woman	Solomon	Daughters of Jerusalem
SEEKING	1:2-4a let us run together		1:4b
	1:5-7 tell me where thou feedest	1:8-10	
(mutual affection)	1:12-14		1:11
	1:16—2:1	1:15	
	2:3-6	2:2	
	2:7		

FINDING	2:8-9
	   Behold, he cometh!
	
	2:10-14
	   (He) said, "Rise up . . . come away"
	
	2:15-17
	   My beloved is mine, and I am his
	
	3:1-4 *(dream)*
	   I sought him
	   I found him		

	3:5		

of seeking and finding? _____

---

4. Compare 2:7 and 3:5 (The same refrain occurs again at 8:4.) Three different translations and interpretations are made of these verses:

(*a*) the Shulamite woman is speaking about Solomon: "till he please" (KJV).

(*b*) Solomon is speaking about the woman: "until she pleases" (NASB).

(*c*) the woman is speaking about love itself "until love itself shall please" (Berkeley). This is the interpretation followed by this manual.

Observe in your Bible that the word *my* (in italics) is not in the original text. So the reference is not the familiar "my love," found in 1:9, 15; 2:2, 10, 13. Consider the context of 2:7 for a clue to its meaning. Note that the picture of 2:6 is one of intimacy between the woman and Solomon (read the verse). Wisely, then, she pleads "not to awaken love prematurely, for love is very tender and easily harmed. At its own proper time it will awaken of itself."[4] Read 3:4-5 and 8:3-4 for the same kind of context. One writer has commented that the words of the Shulamite woman should be written in flaming letters in every hall where young people gather.[5]

III. NOTES

1. "Kiss" (1:2). In the Bible a kiss is an expression of affection, a pledge of peace, a token of reconciliation, or a sign of acceptance. In Canticles it is pure, impassioned affection, not loose infatuation.

2. "Love" (1:2). There are three main root words for *love* found in the Hebrew text of Canticles. They are evenly distributed throughout the book. The first is *ahav* (the usual Old Testament word), which is carried over into the New Testament by *agape* (e.g. 1 Jn 4:8). An example of the use of *ahav* is in 2:4. The second word is *rayah* (e.g. 1:15), which emphasizes the close associative aspect of love. The third word (also translated "beloved"

---

4. Sierd Woudstra, "The Song of Solomon," in *The Wycliffe Bible Commentary*, p. 598.
5. See W. J. Cameron, "The Song of Solomon," in *The New Bible Commentary*.

in KJV) is *dod* (e.g. 1:2), which expresses the intense impulse and desire in a love relationship. (Use an exhaustive concordance to pursue this word study further.)

3. "Wine" (1:2). Wine in the Bible is usually a symbol of the natural delights of men—the joys and the luxuries of earth[6] (cf. Ps 104:15; Joel 3:18; Jn 2:1-10). Recall that wine was the beverage served at the wedding in Cana which Jesus attended (Jn 2:1-11).

4. "I have compared thee . . . to a company of horses" (1:9). This is an example of a passage of Canticles which is understood only if the oriental background is known. (Today, no woman would want to be likened to a horse, no less a company of horses!) The Arabs were known for the very graceful breeds of horses which they reared. So Solomon here may be praising the Shulamite woman's gracefulness. (Note: As you continue your studies in this book, refer to commentaries for help in interpreting unclear statements of this kind.)

5. "Rose of Sharon . . . lily of the valleys" (2:1). This is the only place in the Bible where these flowers are so identified. Note that it is the Shulamite woman (symbolic of the church), not Solomon (symbolic of Christ) who is this rose and lily.[7] "In her humility the bride may think of herself only as a beautiful but humble crocus [rose of Sharon]; he regards her as a lily among thistles."[8]

IV. APPLICATIONS

1. Think about the salvation of a sinner. Who moves first: Christ toward the sinner, or the sinner toward Christ? Compare the following two sets of verses:

"Christ Jesus came into the world to save sinners" (1 Ti 1:15).

"Behold, he cometh" (Song 2:8).

"Come unto me, all ye that labor and are heavy laden, and I will give you rest" (Mt 11:28).

"Rise up . . . and come away" (Song 2:10).

Concerning Matthew 11:28, which is first: the sinner's coming; Christ's giving rest; or the invitation itself?

6. Andrew Miller, *Meditations on The Song of Solomon*, p. 7.
7. Christian songs like "Jesus, Rose of Sharon" are based on the alternate possible view that the speaker of 2:1 is Solomon, not the woman.
8. Woudstra, p. 598.

2. In the story of 1:2—3:5, does the woman, who does the most talking and is identified on Chart L as the seeker, seem to be taking the initiative? Do you think Solomon had opened up this friendship at an earlier time? Recall the setting of the book, discussed in the previous lesson.

3. Keep in mind that Solomon is a type of Christ, and the Shulamite woman is a type of a believer and of the church. What does the passage teach about:

(a) Christ's love for you as a Christian

(b) Christ's love for His church

(c) How you should love Christ

4. Relate the story of this lesson to these words of Jesus: "He that seeketh findeth" (Lk 11:10b). Read Psalm 27.8. With the help of a concordance, read other verses of the Psalms where the word *seek* appears.

5. "My beloved is mine, and I am his" (2:16a). This is a key verse of the Song of Solomon. Ponder its blessed truths as they bear upon your relationship to Christ. The statement is of two parts. Do they mean exactly the same thing? If not, how do they differ?

6. Do many people who accept God's general revelation (e.g. what nature teaches about His attributes) still refuse the special revelation of the gospel of Jesus Christ? Read Matthew 23:37. Contrast such rejection with the Shulamite woman's desire for Solomon.

7. Have you been blessed by other spiritual truths of this passage? (Note: If you have access to the Amplified Bible, answer the questions of its footnotes appearing under these verses: 1:7; 2:6, 13, 14, 15.)

V.   WORDS TO PONDER

His banner over me is love (Song 2:4).

We love him, because he first loved us (1 Jn 4:19).

The Wedding

WE SAW IN THE LAST LESSON

SCENES OF THE COURTSHIP DAYS

OF SOLOMON AND THE SHULAMITE WOMAN.

When she learned of his love for her (2:8-10), she sought him to return that love. And when she found him, she "held on to him and would not let him go" (3:4, NASB). Now the days of wedding and feast have arrived, and we as readers of the Bible text are given the privilege of being onlookers of the bridal procession and guests at the wedding feast.

I. PREPARATION FOR STUDY

1. The marriage customs of Bible lands are much more elaborate than those of the Western culture. Read descriptions of these in a Bible dictionary for a greater appreciation of the passage of this lesson.[1]

2. Read Ephesians 5:23-32. Then read Revelation 19:5-9. The verses of Revelation teach about the marriage of the Lamb (Christ) and His wife (the church). Note that a supper is involved (19:9). This glorious event will take

REVELATION 19:1—20:15   **Chart M**

19:1	19:11	20:1	20:7	20:11 20:15
SONGS MARRIAGE OF THE LAMB	CHRIST'S RETURN TO EARTH WAR: ARMAGEDDON	MILLENNIUM (CHRIST'S REIGN ON EARTH)	SATAN'S LOOSING WAR: GOG AND MAGOG	GREAT WHITE THRONE JUDGMENT (ALL UNBELIEVERS)

1. An excellent article is to be found in *The New Bible Dictionary*, pages 788-91.

place in the end times, after the church has been raptured to be with Christ. Chart M shows the sequence of events after the marriage supper of the Lamb, as taught by Revelation 19:1—20:15.

II. ANALYSIS

Passage to be analyzed: 3:6—5:1

Stanza divisions: at verses 3:6; 4:1, 7, 16; 5:1a, 1b. Mark these in your Bible.

Chart N shows the pattern of this dialogue. Observe that it moves through one complete cycle, thus:

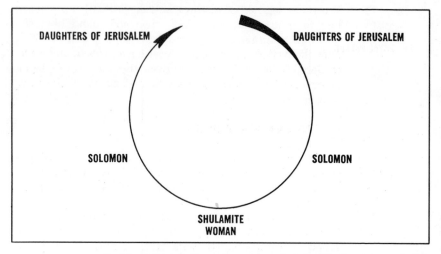

1. Key phrases have been recorded inside the boxes of this chart. Underline these phrases in your Bible. Do this for other key words and phrases in the course of your study.
2. Observe that this passage is of two main parts:
(a) The bridal pair enters Jerusalem
(b) At the wedding feast in the royal palace
3. "In the day of his espousals" (3:11) is translated "on the day of his wedding" in New American Standard Bible. The tone of the entire verse points to the wedding of Solomon and the Shulamite woman, not to a former marriage of Solomon to another bride.
4. The concluding phrase "eat . . . drink . . . O lovers" (5:1b, NASB) suggests the setting of wedding feast.

THE WEDDING
Song of Solomon (3:6—5:1)

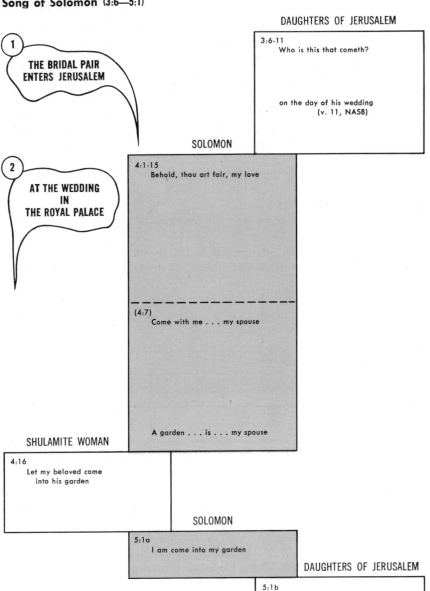

DAUGHTERS OF JERUSALEM

1 THE BRIDAL PAIR ENTERS JERUSALEM

3:6-11
Who is this that cometh?

on the day of his wedding
(v. 11, NASB)

SOLOMON

2 AT THE WEDDING IN THE ROYAL PALACE

4:1-15
Behold, thou art fair, my love

(4:7)
Come with me . . . my spouse

A garden . . . is . . . my spouse

SHULAMITE WOMAN

4:16
Let my beloved come
into his garden

SOLOMON

5:1a
I am come into my garden

DAUGHTERS OF JERUSALEM

5:1b
Eat . . . drink . . . O lovers
(NASB)

5. The bridegroom's praise of the bride, in 4:1-15, was the kind of song which was sung at the wedding feast. This is still a custom in many weddings of the Near East today.

6. Note that Solomon is the main speaker of this passage. This is the way it should be, for he, as the man, takes the initiative, and is the head and spokesman of the new household.

7. Note the repeated appearance of the word *come* on the chart. Read the verses in the context of the Bible text. Observe how the *personal, voluntary* character of the wedding is emphasized by this:

> "Come with me . . . my spouse" (4-8)—*invitation*
> "Let my beloved come into his garden" (4:16)—response *and invitation*
> "I am come into my garden" (5:1a)—*response*

The bride was not obligated to marry Solomon, nor was she enlisted by his parents, as many brides were chosen in those days.

8. Observe the four appearances of the word *garden* in 4:12, 16; 5:1a. In your own words, expand on the meanings shown below.

text	meaning
4:12 SOLOMON: "A garden inclosed is . . . my spouse"	My bride is a garden
4:16 SHULAMITE: "Blow upon my garden"	Blow upon me
4:16 SHULAMITE: "Let my beloved come into my garden"	Let Solomon come to me
5:1 SOLOMON: "I am come into my garden"	I come to you

9. What is the bride's prominent thought at the wedding? (4:16) _____

10. What is the bridegroom's prominent thought at the wedding? (5:1a) _____

III. NOTES

1. "His bed" (3:7). The New American Standard Bible paraphrases this as Solomon's "traveling couch."
2. "Daughters of Zion" (3:11). This term usually refers to the women of the entire city of Jerusalem.[2] The smaller group, "daughters of Jerusalem," addresses these words to the larger group.
3. "The crown wherewith his mother crowned him" (3:11). This was not a royal but a festive crown, a wedding coronet of gold and silver, which bridegrooms as well as brides wore at Israelitish weddings.[3] Solomon's mother was Bathsheba.
4. "Your hair is like a flock of goats" (4:1). The bride probably had dark, wavy hair. (Refer to a commentary for interpretations of the other metaphors of this song of praise.)

IV. APPLICATIONS

The following questions (except the last) are based on the interpretation that the wedding of Solomon and the Shulamite woman prefigures the Christian's entrance into union with Christ at conversion. For each question, try to identify what part of the Bible text cited is being referred to by the question.

A. 3:6-11. Should Christian friends and relatives rejoice over the conversion of a loved one? Should such rejoicing ever diminish?

B. 4:1-15. Do you think Christ loves you, one of His own, as intensely as the love prefigured by Solomon's words of these verses? Can you think of passages in the Bible which speak of His love? What was the greatest expression of His love?

C. 4:8. Compare this verse with 1 Peter 5:8. Does your spiritual union with Christ mean that you are never tempted to compromise with the world? Compare "Come with me . . . from the dens of lions" (4:8) with Romans 12:2.

2. See footnote of Berkeley Version.
3. Otto Zockler, "The Song of Solomon," in *Commentary on the Holy Scriptures*, ed. John Peter Lange, p. 84.

D. 4:16. Should a Christian surrender all of his being to Christ? Compare Romans 12:1. Why is total consecration the only way to blessed communion with Christ?

E. 5:1b. Is the Christian life supposed to be a joyful one? Read Philippians 4:4-7. You may want to read Paul's entire letter to the Philippians, where joy is the keynote.

F. In what ways will the marriage supper of the Lamb (Rev 19:5-9) be the perfect fulfillment of this passage of the Song of Solomon?

G. Before leaving this lesson, apply the text figuratively to God and Israel, as the original readers of the book would have done. According to this interpretation, Israel is the bride, and God the Bridegroom. Read Hosea 2:16, 18-20; and Ezekiel 16:8-14. From your recollection of Old Testament history, did God manifest His love to Israel over and over again, even when Israel spurned that love?

V. WORDS TO PONDER

The love of Jesus,
    what it is,
        none but His loved ones know.

BERNARD OF CLAIRVAUX

A Troubled Dream
of Separation

COMMUNION WITH CHRIST IS NOT

A STATIC RELATIONSHIP; DAILY IT IS

TESTED AND TRIED, TO MAKE IT DEEPER.

Soon after her marriage to Solomon, the Shulamite woman dreamed of an experience that alienated her and Solomon, bringing her agony of soul until there was reunion. The passage of this lesson illustrates some very important spiritual truths about broken fellowship with Christ. It is the dark picture of the Song of Solomon, but what you learn from it can be of great blessing to your own life.

I. PREPARATION FOR STUDY

Refer again to the survey Chart K. Note the outline that divides the Song of Solomon into two main parts:

1.2	5:2	8:14
Love first expressed and experienced	Love tried and triumphant	

The passage of this lesson begins the last half of the book. As noted above, the theme of the passage is the trial, or proving, of love. You may recall a similar truth which Peter wrote in his epistle, about the trying of faith: "That the trial of your faith, being much more precious than of gold that perisheth, though it be tried with fire, might be found unto praise and honour and glory at the appearing of Jesus Christ" (1 Pe 1:7).

Note that the proving is meant to bring about the approving.

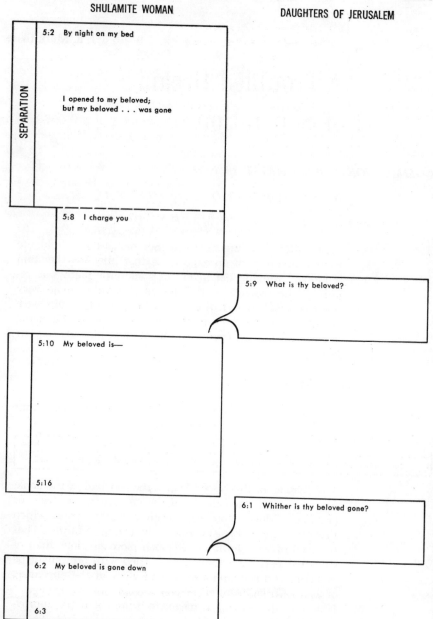

SHULAMITE WOMAN

DAUGHTERS OF JERUSALEM

SEPARATION

5:2 By night on my bed

I opened to my beloved;
but my beloved . . . was gone

5:8 I charge you

5:9 What is thy beloved?

5:10 My beloved is—

5:16

6:1 Whither is thy beloved gone?

6:2 My beloved is gone down

6:3

II. ANALYSIS

Passage to be analyzed: 5:2—6:3

Stanza divisions: at verses 5:2, 8, 9, 10; 6:1, 2. Mark these in your Bible.

Chart O is a worksheet for analysis of this passage. Use it as you used the similar worksheets of the previous lessons.

1. Who is the main speaker of this passage?

2. The first line of 5:2 is the basis for calling this a dream. (If it was a waking experience, the spiritual applications are the same.) Some interpret only verses 2-7 as the dream itself. If that were the case, one wonders why the Shulamite woman would seek help after she awoke (5:8), since she knew the separation from her lover was only a dream. If 5:8 is part of the dream, then are also all the verses that follow, to the end of the passage (6:3).

3. Read "sick of love" (5:8) as "lovesick."

4. The word to emphasize in 5:9 is "so": "that thou dost *so* charge us." What do the daughters of Jerusalem mean by 5:9?

5. Compare the woman's praise of Solomon (5:10-16) with his praise of her at the wedding feast (4:1-15). _____

_____

6. What is the response of the daughters of Jerusalem (6:1)? _____.

_____

Do the words, "that we may seek him with thee" suggest that they wanted to find Solomon for their own good as well as for the woman's? _____

_____

7. Compare 6:2-3 with 5:6. _____

_____

Before, the Shulamite woman did not know where Solomon was. Now she does. Can you account for the change (cf. 4:16; 5:1a)? _____

8. Note on the left-hand side of Chart O that the word *separation* identifies the contents of 5:2-7. Complete this outline for the other two stanzas where there are blank spaces.

9. Spend more time studying the details of 5:2-7, since these verses are crucial in the story.

(a) Had Solomon been away (5:2)? _____
Must this suggest unfaithfulness on his part? (Remember that Solomon was king of a large kingdom. Compare the extensive journeys of the president of the United States today.)

(*b*) What was Solomon's request (5:2)? _____

_____

(*c*) Does verse 3 suggest delay, or hesitation, on the

woman's part? _____

(*d*) What caused the woman to get up to open the door

(5:4-5)? _____

_____

(*e*) What did she find (5:6)? _____

III. NOTES

Refer to *The New Bible Commentary* for symbolic meanings of many of the phrases of this passage.

1. "By the hole of the door" (5:4). "Eastern houses had an aperture above the lock for the insertion of the key, which was large enough to admit the hand. There might also be an opening through which the occupant of an apartment might look and speak."[1]

2. "He is altogether lovely" (5:16). A literal translation is, "All of him is delightful." The same word "lovely" appears in 2 Samuel 1:23.

3. "I am my beloved's, and my beloved is mine" (6:3). This verse inspired the writing of the following stanza of a favorite hymn by George Robinson:

> His forever, only His;
> Who the Lord and me shall part?

1. W. J. Cameron, "Song of Solomon," in *The New Bible Commentary*, p. 552.

Ah, with what a rest of bliss
Christ can fill the loving heart.
Heav'n and earth may fade and flee,
First-born light in gloom decline;
But while God and I shall be,
I am His, and He is mine.

IV. APPLICATIONS

We will assume that the location of the account of the dream in Canticles—*after* the wedding—is intended to direct the spiritual application to the regenerate soul who has been brought into union with Christ. His union with Christ (state) is the basis for constant, conscious communion with Christ (condition). This is consistent with our earlier applications, shown here:

1:2	3:6	5:2	8:14
COURTSHIP DAYS	WEDDING	MARRIED LIFE	
sinner introduced to Christ	union with Christ at conversion	communion with Christ in the Christian life	

Note that union is before communion.

A. 5:2. Is your spiritual communion with Christ, now that you are saved, a forced relationship? Would you say that in a real sense Christ continually knocks at the door of your heart (Rev 3:20), desiring intimate fellowship with you (cf. Jn 10:9)? Are you responsible to open this door, even as you let Christ into your heart when you were saved?

A very interesting conversation between Jesus and Peter is recorded in the gospel of John. Read John 21:15-19. The word *lovest* spoken by Jesus in verses 15 and 16, is *agapas*, which has the meaning of unselfish love, ready to serve. The words *lovest* (v. 17) and *love* (vv. 15-17) are *fileis* and *filo*, which suggest intimate and tender affection.[2] What kind of love does Jesus want to receive from you?

B. 5:3. Is there *any* excuse for not wanting, or for postponing Christ's fellowship?

C. 5:6. Why do you think Christ would absent Himself from a seeker in a situation like this? What is involved here: broken fellowship or lost salvation? What would Christ be trying to teach His beloved one? Is this a trying experience for the Christian? Are prayers of saints not answered if they pray at their convenience and on their own terms?

Apply this passage to God and Israel, in Old Testament times. Read Isaiah 54:5-8 and observe that the Lord speaks to His bride about His having to forsake her for a short season. What reason is given? Read the psalmist's prayer, "Leave me not, neither forsake me," in Psalm 27:9.

D. 6:2-3. What is the condition which restores fellowship between a believer and Christ? How do verses 5:10—6:3 reveal that the Shulamite woman's heart was made right, bringing her into renewed communion with Solomon? (Note that at 6:4 ff. she is with Solomon again.)

V. WORDS TO PONDER

> O Love that wilt not let me go,
> I rest my weary soul in Thee;
> I give Thee back the life I owe,
> That in Thine ocean depths its flow
> may richer, fuller be.

GEORGE MATHESON

---

2. See Irving L. Jensen, *John*, of this self-study series (Chicago: Moody, 1970), p. 105.

The Triumph of True Love

THE LAST CHAPTERS OF CANTICLES REVEAL THAT THE ESTRANGEMENT DESCRIBED BY 5:6, WHETHER REAL OR VISIONARY, WAS ONLY TEMPORARY.

In this passage we learn that the restored love relationship between Solomon and the Shulamite woman grew stronger with time and experience, and was bound with a seal of heart devotion.

I. PREPARATION FOR STUDY

Chart P is an excerpt of the survey Chart K. Study this as the context of the passage of this lesson.

CONTEXT OF 6:4—8:14   **Chart P**

LOVE TRIED AND TRIUMPHANT		
5:2	6:4	8:5 8:14
a troubled dream of separation	mutual love of husband and wife	the seal of their love

This lesson

II. ANALYSIS

Segments to be analyzed: 6:4—8:4 and 8:5-14
Stanza divisions: at verses 6:4, 11, 13a, 13b; 7:1, 9b; 8:4, 5a, 5b, 8, 10, 13, 14. Mark these in your Bible.
Study this passage in two units, as shown on Chart P. Use the worksheets of Chart Q and Chart R to record your

MUTUAL LOVE OF HUSBAND AND WIFE 6:4—8:4

SHULAMITE WOMAN   SOLOMON   DAUGHTERS OF JERUSALEM

6:4-10

THOU ART BEAUTIFUL

6:11-12

I went down into the garden

6:13a

6:13b

7:1-9a

HOW BEAUTIFUL!

7:9b—8:4

Come, my beloved,
let us go forth

8:4

STIR NOT UP

SHULAMITE WOMAN	SOLOMON	DAUGHTERS OF JERUSALEM

8:5a

8:5b-7

SET ME AS A SEAL
UPON THY HEART

8:8-9

8:10-12

8:13

Thy voice:
Cause me to hear it.

8:14

MAKE HASTE, MY BELOVED

observations, just as you used the worksheets of previous lessons. (Note: move from top to bottom, according to the progression of verses. Begin in the middle column for Chart Q, and in the right-hand column for Chart R.) The procedure to follow in using work sheets like these is simple yet basic:

1. During the course of your study record any key words or phrases which strike you as being significant. Record them approximately in the correct location inside the stanza's box. (Examples are given.)

2. After you have finished this phase of recording, such things as outlines, progressions, and comparisons, may begin to appear as you reflect on what you have already recorded of the Bible text. Print those outlines, etc., outside the boxes.

It was noted in an earlier lesson that there is no discernible drama of action in any particular passage of the Song of Solomon. So do not be discouraged if you cannot arrive at such things as outlines for this book, referred to above. The important thing is to record key words and phrases. The study phase of reflection and application depends much on what key words and phrases you observe in the text.

Analyze these two passages similar to the projects of the previous lessons. Let Chart Q and Chart R serve as reference points throughout your study. Some questions on applications are given later in the lesson.

III. NOTES

1. "My soul made me like the chariots" (6:12). A possible reading is paraphrased as, "I was stricken with terrible desire to sit beside my beloved in his chariot."[1]

2. "What will ye see . . . two armies?" (6:13b). The New American Standard Bible translates 6:13b thus: "Why should you gaze at the Shulamite, as at the dance of the two companies?" The Hebrew word for "two armies" is *Mahanaim*, hence the Berkeley Version rendering, "as she dances the Mahanaim dance." Woudstra comments, "The Mahanaim dance must have been a well-known dance.

1. See *The Living Bible*, p. 532, fn. (d).

Mahanaim was a place located on the boundary of the tribe of Gad, not far from the river Jordan."[2]

3. "I am my beloved's, and his desire is toward me" (7:10). Compare the similar statements of 2:16 and 6:3. Robert Lee comments on the differences:

> a. At first the ruling thought of the soul is "My Beloved is mine and I am His," (2:16). At this stage we think chiefly of Christ as ours, and in some way for our pleasure.
> b. Then we come to "I am my Beloved's, and my Beloved is mine," (6:3). His ownership takes first place in our thoughts.
> c. At last we come to "I am my Beloved's and His desire is toward me" (7:10), where the word "mine" is altogether dropped in the perfect assurance that to be His includes all.[3]

4. "Stir not up" (8:4). Recall this similar charge in 2:7 and 3:5, and the verse preceding each.

5. "A seal upon thine heart" (8:6). The seal was a signet ring or bracelet, worn on the right hand (8:6; cf. Jer 22:24) or hung by a string around the neck. It was a symbol of preciousness and authority, and would remind Solomon of his wife when he was away from her.[4]

6. "She hath no breasts" (8:8). That is, she had not reached maturity.

7. "If she be a wall . . . a door" (8:9). Some commentators see the wall as symbolizing chastity (keeping suitors at a proper distance), and the door symbolizing the opposite (yielding to their advances). Throughout the Song of Solomon, the Shulamite woman appears to be a chaste and pure woman.

IV. SELECTED APPLICATIONS

A. 7:10-12. How does the phrase "Let us" symbolize the close relation of husband and wife in all of their living? Apply this to your relationship to Christ in your daily walk.

B. 8:6. What is the spiritual significance of a seal, as far as relationship to Christ is concerned? In what sense is Christ a seal upon your heart and upon your arm? Read

---

2. Sierd Woudstra, "Song of Solomon," in *The Wycliffe Bible Commentary*, p. 602.
3. Robert Lee, *The Outlined Bible*, comments on 7:10.
4. Many commentators interpret 8:6 as being spoken by the woman, not Solomon.

John 3:36. Do you see assurance and guarantee in the phrase "hath everlasting life"?

C. 8:13. This is the last recorded message spoken by Solomon in his book. He wanted to hear the voice of his wife continually. Does Christ want to hear your voice? What New Testament passages speak of this?

D. 8:14. The last recorded words of the young wife are the yearning that Solomon make haste to return. Solomon was probably away on business. "Come quickly, my beloved." Compare this with the closing verses of the book of Revelation, especially 22:17, 20. Is this the ruling desire of your heart? Why did Jesus leave this earth and go to heaven?

*   *   *

A Concluding Thought

The Song of Solomon, in its spiritual applications for the Christian, dwells mostly on the new experience of regeneration in the life of a believer, as he is united with Christ and enters into glorious communion with the lover of his soul. The book's main message is that life *with* Christ and life *in* Christ has a deep and satisfying joy now, today. Paul wrote much about this in Ephesians, a book whose theme is Christ and the church. The word *now* is inserted in the following verses of Ephesians, to emphasize this present aspect of communion with Christ:

> For this cause I bow my knees unto the Father of our Lord Jesus Christ . . . that he would grant you, according to the riches of his glory, to be strengthened [NOW] with might by his Spirit in the inner man; that Christ may dwell [NOW] in your hearts by faith; that ye, being rooted and grounded in love, may [NOW] be able to comprehend with all saints what is the breadth, and length, and depth, and height; and to know [NOW] the love of Christ, which passeth knowledge, that ye might be filled [NOW] with all the fullness of God (Eph 3:14, 16-19).

But the joys of communion with Christ now are only a foretaste of the glories yet to come, when Christ returns for His own. That is why the final strain of the Song of Solomon, the best of songs, is this beautiful prayer, "Make haste, my beloved!" (8:14).

> In mansions of glory and endless delight,
> I'll ever adore Thee in heaven so bright;
> I'll sing with the glittering crown on my brow,
> If ever I loved Thee, my Jesus, 'tis now.

WILLIAM R. FEATHERSTONE

Selected Sources for Further Study

A. *Commentaries on Ecclesiastes*

Chambers, Oswald. *Shade of His Hand*. London: Simpkin Marshall, 1941.

Delitzsch, Franz. *Commentary on The Song of Songs and Ecclesiastes*. Grand Rapids: Eerdmans, 1950. Technical treatment of the Hebrew text.

Hendry, G. S. "Ecclesiastes." In *The New Bible Commentary*, ed. F. Davidson. Grand Rapids: Eerdman, 1953.

Laurin, Robert. "Ecclesiastes." In *The Wycliffe Bible Commentary*, ed. Charles F. Pfeiffer and Everett F. Harrison. Chicago: Moody, 1962.

Leupold, H. C. *Exposition of Ecclesiastes*. Grand Rapids: Baker, 1952.

McNeile, A. H. *An Introduction to Ecclesiastes*. Cambridge: University, 1904.

Rankin, O. S. "The Book of Ecclesiastes." In *The Interpreter's Bible*. Vol. 5. New York: Abingdon, 1956.

B. *Commentaries on The Song of Solomon*

Adeney, Walter F. "The Song of Solomon." In *The Expositors' Bible*, ed. W. Robertson Nicoll. New York: Eaton & Maine, n.d.

Cameron, W. J. "Song of Solomon." In *The New Bible Commentary*, ed. F. Davidson. Grand Rapids: Eerdmans, 1953.

Ironside, H. A. *Addresses on the Song of Solomon*. New York: Loizeaux, n.d.

La Botz, Paul. *The Romance of the Ages*. Grand Rapids: Kregel, 1965.

Taylor, J. Hudson. *Union and Communion*. London: China Inland Mission, 1914.

Woudstra, Sierd. "Song of Solomon." In *The Wycliffe Bible Commentary*, ed. Charles F. Pfeiffer and Everett F. Harrison. Chicago: Moody, 1962.

Zockler, Otto. "The Song of Solomon." In *Commentary on the Holy Scriptures*, ed. John Peter Lange. Reprint. Grand Rapids: Zondervan, n.d.

C. *General References*

Amplified Bible. Grand Rapids: Zondervan, 1965.

Archer, Gleason L. *A Survey of Old Testament Introduction*. Chicago: Moody, 1964.

Douglas, J. D., ed. *The New Bible Dictionary*. Grand Rapids: Eerdmans, 1962.

Jensen, Irving L. *Independent Bible Study*. Chicago: Moody, 1963.

The Living Bible. Wheaton: Tyndale, 1971.

New American Standard Bible. Text ed. Chicago: Moody, 1972.

New Scofield Reference Bible. New York: Oxford, 1967.

Oesterley, W. O. E. *The Wisdom of Egypt and the Old Testament*. New York: Macmillan, 1927.

Strong, James. *The Exhaustive Concordance of the Bible*. New York: Abingdon, 1890.

Tenney, Merrill C., ed. *The Zondervan Pictorial Bible Dictionary*. Grand Rapids: Zondervan, 1963.

Unger, Merrill F. *Unger's Bible Handbook*. Chicago: Moody, 1966.

Young, Edward J. *An Introduction to the Old Testament*. Rev. ed. Grand Rapids: Eerdmans, 1958.

Young, Robert. *Analytical Concordance to the Bible*. Grand Rapids: Eerdmans, n.d.